THE
IDEATION
EQUATION

HOW A HANDFUL OF HABITS
CAN MAKE YOU A CREATIVE GENIUS

LINUS BILLE

Before we begin...

Hi there! Thank you for picking up this book!
To make the most out of the experience ahead, please
go to **ideationequation.com**, and check out all the free
complimentary content I have made available for you. For
example, all of the illustrations in this book (and then some) are
included in a PowerPoint file, so that you can always access
relevant concepts at work, or indeed anywhere.

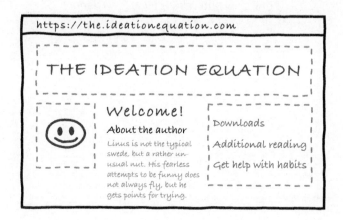

Dedication

For Jenna. You are my greatest inspiration.

For Leon and Miliam. You are my two best ideas.

For Daniel. Literally, for you, my friend.

Acknowledgements

A big **THANK YOU** to all of the amazing people that helped me make this book into something of which I am extremely proud! I would like to take the opportunity to mention a few people that made especially valuable contributions:

1st Editor: Christopher Morris
2nd Editor: Lauren Squillino
Cover art: Afra Noubarzade

(All other illustrations were proudly made by the author himself...)

Book interior design: Eisen Adorador

Author's Advisory Board:
Bianca Welds
David J. W. Bailey
Ernesto Gutiérrez
Jorge Ignacio Blanco Lopez
Karin Andersson
Katarina Nordström
Magnus Envall
Matteo Tassi
Michael Hönger
Wellington Holbrook

A special thank you also goes out to my partners in Eicorn for supporting me on this journey.

Preface

"Linus, how is it that you are able to consistently and reliably think outside the box, and come up with such original ideas?"

I did not have an immediate answer to this question, that came from my good friend Daniel. But the query triggered an intellectual journey to find some answers, which eventually resulted in this book. I started to write partly to structure my own thinking and learning, and partly to provide Daniel with a good response to his question, an answer that went beyond the platitude of 'being born with a creative personality'.

This short background story reveals what sort of audience I had in mind as I started to write, long before the idea to create an entire book was born: an audience of one, namely Daniel Borg. He is one of the most intelligent people I have ever met, with a reading habit that far surpasses my own, and an attention to detail that leaves nothing to chance.

He is also a very analytical thinker, and more influenced by logical arguments than anything else.

But he felt that he should, at the time of asking, try to develop a more creative side to his sharp intellect, a side he felt that I not only merely possessed, but had also mastered. I would argue that, as I write these words, he is very well on his way!

I have myself, without a doubt, also become even better at ideation and outside-the-box thinking on this journey, largely because I can better control the beliefs and habits that underpin my own creative thinking ability. The reason for this is that by thinking about thinking, for years essentially, I now have a much better understanding of why my creative intellectual abilities were quite good to begin with.

By helping Daniel, and cross-referencing with others as this project matured, I could also see how a few core themes, consistent with scientific findings, emerged as general advice for each and every person interested in becoming a more creative thinker. Inclusively, these core themes make up *The Ideation Equation.*

But before we dive into that, I think you as a reader will benefit from knowing a bit more about me as a writer, and, specifically, about my disposition to write about ideation. For most of my career, which at the time of writing is passing the 25-year mark, I have been an entrepreneur and innovator. Initially, in the entertainment industry working with music and film production, and later in fintech and other digital technologies. But I have also worked for many years as a consultant, helping mostly large firms with Swedish origins with their innovation initiatives.

During the first 15 years of building businesses and advising corporate clients, my thinking was what I would call 'archetypical' for a creative autodidact. I made most decisions based on the law of attraction, I evolved through constant trial and error, I was fearless (I still am), and I had a clear bias for action - to just try something, and see if it would work. I was, arguably, quite successful, as many self-taught creative thinkers and practitioners are.

But I felt that something was missing - a deeper understanding of why I 'knew' how certain things concerning innovation would work, and other things would not. So I decided to go back to school, and take things more seriously this time than I had in my late teens and early twenties, which led me to the Executive MBA program at Saïd Business School, the University of Oxford.

This changed my life completely, because it inspired me to transform my way of thinking. While at Oxford, I understood, for the first time, the inherent power and value of the scientific method.

I should include a disclaimer immediately that I do not necessarily mean the current academic interpretation of how to conduct science, because I think that process has become disturbingly corrupted by dysfunctional incentives (an opinion to develop in another book...). Rather, the notion that the world runs on invisible rules and probabilities, and that there are ways, a set of tools we call 'the scientific method', to find out what those rules and probabilities are, at least approximately.

When this insight firmly grabbed hold of me, it no longer made any sense to make decisions based on passion, or to more or less mindlessly try things and supposedly learn from the outcome, which most of the time would result in some sort of failure.

I also discovered that other people around the world had started to use the scientific method to boost innovation efforts, some quite superficially, such as Eric Ries with his *Lean Startup* (Crown Business, 2011) methodology, while others were taking a more orthodox scientific approach, for example Arnaldo Camuffo et al with their *Scientific Approach to Entrepreneurial Decision Making* (Management Science, 2019).

I myself started the innovation consulting company Eicorn with a friend, with the ambition of bringing evidence-based innovation practices to large organisations. Eicorn's mission is to help its clients to better understand and use reality's hidden rules and probabilities, underpinning how new things come to life and grow, and in the process make an impact on the world. Our hypothesis is that, on a planet in dire need of innovative solutions to an avalanche of cataclysmic problems, helping many innovators do better will have a bigger impact than just trying to solve one of those problems ourselves.

At Eicorn, I met Daniel for the first time. He was the fourth person in and is, at the time of writing, a partner in the firm. Although, these days we are first and foremost friends, and business partners second. He issued his question about how I am able to think outside the box and come up with new ideas, already several years ago; and I have since then been thinking, researching, learning and writing bits and pieces of *The Ideation Equation* every now and then, in what can only be described as a fairly lame tempo!

Then, one late summer day in 2022, something happened that made me accelerate my effort. Daniel called me, asking me to calmly listen to everything he had to say, and to refrain from panicking halfway through. He told me he had been in an accident, that he was calling me from the trauma ward of the university hospital, and that he had multiple unstable fractures in his spine, alongside a broken shoulder and collarbone, and several shattered ribs. Doctors had put 12 titanium screws and 3 plates in his back, and estimated that he had a decent chance of regaining some sort of normal functioning again, in time.

Daniel did not explicitly ask me that day to provide a deeper and more holistic answer to his, by now years old, question about how to think outside the box and have more creative ideas. But this incident drove me to focus more on the matter. And soon, the idea was born that all of these articles and explorations that I had produced around this topic, for Daniel to learn from, could become the core teachings of a book!

After writing a few complementary sections, and compiling a first draft, I invited some of my brightest friends to read it, and give me advice on how to turn that first draft into the final manuscript that you are reading now. I owe them, as well as my awesome editor and writing coach Chris, and my always supportive and loving wife Jenna, a great deal; and will be forever grateful for their enthusiasm, generosity, and intellectual honesty.

Introduction

While all of the core concepts and insights of my original texts were meant solely for Daniel, this book is compiled for *you*, with the intention of supporting your personal journey towards more creative thinking! Due to its origin, as a personal mentoring device of sorts, it is not the typical business and leadership book that claims to solve all kinds of innovation issues for managers, teams and big corporations.

Therefore, this book is refreshingly, if I may say so myself, free from corporate innovation anecdotes that you have no doubt already heard far too many times - the stories, and collapses, of Kodak, Blockbuster, Facit, Borders, and so on. Rather, my aim is to help you, as an individual, super-charge the source of all good ideas - your thought-process, and its habitat, your brain.

I'm not going to question the widespread idea that some

people are born with more inherent creativity than others, because that is probably true. But I am going to demonstrate that there is another path to big thinking - one that is available to anyone and everyone! Today, this alternative path is increasingly enlightened by science. Perhaps not in terms of answering exactly what constitutes creativity, but definitely in terms of mapping out what people can do to become more original thinkers.

Truly creative ideas are often perceived as having appeared magically, sometimes even to the people that conceived them. This is perhaps understandable, and is even perpetuated by stories such as Archimedes infamously, and possibly apocryphally, screaming "Eureka!" ("I have found it") in the bath. But although the process of creativity may begin as a surprise, the assumption that ideas emanate and originate from nowhere is a myth.

The general idea behind *The Ideation Equation* is very straightforward. It is grounded in the philosophy referred to as a 'growth mindset', which basically states that we can learn anything. Even though we are born with different base rates of creative thinking skills, it has been scientifically proven in every conceivable fashion that ideation can be learned. And, perhaps more importantly, that ideation is an innate ability that can be both suppressed and amplified depending on our beliefs and habits.

Examining one's ability to conceive great ideas from this angle, the process very much resembles physical abilities with which we are more familiar. And from that physical ability, we can extend the analogy to an activity that goes beyond the ability itself, such as playing a sport.

For example, you can kick a ball, as long as you are not born with any physical disabilities that prevent you from doing so. The same principle applies to ideas - you can have them if you can think. However, when it comes to intellectual abilities and our development over time, these facets of our composition are incredibly hard to measure and compare with other people. There is nothing like a golf handicap score in the world of creative thinking; IQ scores do not even come remotely close. Measuring intelligence, or the ability to think, in any sort of qualitative way is incredibly challenging.

Consequently, it is very easy for us to compare our ideation abilities with masters in the field of thinking creatively, and feel that we 'do not have what it takes'. This is a big mistake that I believe people would avoid if they considered creative thinking to be more like a sport. The great thinkers that people compare themselves with do not just 'kick a ball', they play mental football at a professional level! You would not compare your ball-kicking abilities to Lionel Messi or Pernille Harder (unless you were Zlatan), would you?

First, you have to do the work that they have invested to become that good, and then you can think about comparing. And, by the way, if you cannot relate to football as an analogy, just replace the word 'football' with 'dancing', 'skateboarding' or 'chess'; you will see that the logic holds true regardless.

The question of whether masters are born or made is probably as old as the concept of mastery itself. And the answer is - both. But an increasing amount of general evidence suggests that the honing of skills weighs heavier than innate talent. It is also becoming increasingly evident that we learn to master such skills through mentoring from other masters, rather than via our own repeated failures.

One example of this is the inaccuracy of predictions made by sports agents about which young talents are going to be future stars. These predictions are notoriously unreliable, which suggests that what the less talented, but more motivated and better mentored, youngsters invest in practice and development on their way to mastery has a greater impact than raw talent.

Even outside of traditional sports, there are examples of competitors who defy conventions, coming to the fore thanks to their own determination. For example, the highest ranked chess player in the world at the time of writing, Magnus Carlsen, is widely considered to be the greatest chess player of all-time, and has won the world championship five times. Yet his reason for being interested in chess was quite prosaic; he kept losing to his sister, and decided to learn how to beat her. And so he did, and then some!

One can interpret this as both good and bad news. The good news is that if you feel hopelessly incapable of thinking outside the box, you probably have not practised enough. The bad news is that you have a lot of hard work in front of you!

Actually, there is an additional piece of *good* news. Knowing that practice matters more than raw talent also means that you can expect tangible results, as long as you do the right exercises. Thinking in terms of "what if I spend all this time trying to become more creative, but see no progress?" makes no sense, given what we know about the development of human abilities. In essence, we know that investing effort *does* result in improved attainment.

But, of course, the key phrase in the previous paragraph is 'the right exercises', and this is to a great extent why I believe that this book needed to be written, not only for Daniel, but also for a much larger audience. As an innovation consultant (among many other things), I am ashamed to admit that the mainstream tools that exist in my industry in this area are exceedingly poor.

Coming back to the football analogy, to become a great player you need to understand the game of football, know the rules of football, master countless football moves, exercise the muscles that are utilised in football, eat and drink appropriate food for building the ideal physique to play football, and so on.

But most existing books, courses, podcasts, and memes about ideation would prepare you better for curling, basketball or surfing; in short, they are not capable of doing the job that you require from them. Conversely, with this book, my ambition is to provide a detailed road to ideation mastery. And one that really works! To justify such a bold claim, I believe that some clarifications are in order.

Firstly, I would distinguish very clearly between coming up with an idea and realising it. One of the problems with most existing ideation frameworks is that they blend these two aspects of innovation, which are sometimes referred to as 'first creation' and 'second creation'. This common lack of distinction between the two elements of ideation often results in people attempting to implement ideas that are still too immature, or, simply put, not good enough!

My focus with this book is not to teach the A to Z of innovative entrepreneurship, from zero to billionaire, or anything like that. It is simply, and only, ideation from the perspective of the individual. I recognise, of course, that the development of ideas is an iterative process between creating and building, but the focus of this book is on the internal process required to come up with great ideas - no more, no less.

Secondly, so much of the advice offered by management consultants and business gurus about creativity and ideation is based on hearsay and anecdotes. And sometimes, even worse, false or invalid evidence! During my research for this work, I read several recently published books on the subject of creativity and ideation, that cited, for example, Neuro-Linguistic Programming (NLP) methods (mostly pseudoscience), and that contained long arguments about behavioural priming (largely invalidated) and the Dunning-Kruger effect (unclear causation) as evidence for the ideas presented and techniques taught. In many cases, a critical read will even reveal that the 'evidence' provided has no clear connection to the claim made by the author.

If we operated in the world of football, these 'coaches' would quickly be out of a job, and their books would be taken off the shelves. Because in any sport, performance and results can be readily assessed and compared. But in the world of creativity, the rules are unclear; indeed, some might say that there are no rules. Progress can be superficial, and yet celebrated - "just look at all those colourful stickies!" - and the gurus are mostly selected based on association (such as 'ex-Google', 'ex-Tesla', 'ex-Apple'), rather than on real influence.

Thirdly, unlike almost all of my peers in this industry, I do not profess to offer any quick fixes or shortcuts. Instead, what I would advocate is a course of hard work invested in the right things, which will help you to progress, and, ultimately, achieve mastery.

Again, the sports analogy makes perfect sense. Tell me a sport (worth playing) that you can start practising in the morning and reach full proficiency in the afternoon? I cannot think of anything even close to this! Yet, this is exactly what many corporate creativity workshop gurus will offer you. "Trust the process," they will tell you.

That is like a coach telling you to trust the gameplan, when it is time to play a football championship final, but you have done zero preparation. What will matter most - that supposed gameplan, or how prepared you are for the game? The answer is obvious!

With those harsh words having been directed at my own guild, I will from hereon try to leave further criticism and evaluation of what others do out of this book, and go back to focusing on *you* and *your creative thinking*.

After reading this text, you will have an understanding of how ideation is indeed similar to an equation. There are five activities, or factors, that determine success, and many different actions you can take to improve your performance within each of these critical factors.

While reading, I encourage you to take notes, and especially focus on the areas where you feel the least confident. In common with an athlete, these are the areas where you should primarily focus your training - a method sometimes referred to as 'deliberate practice'. As soon as you have trained yourself to a higher level of performance within one of those areas that requires improvement, you move on to your new least proficient skill, in a never-ending loop of continuous improvement.

What those five activities are, and how they fit together, will become clear to you as you advance through the book. But what you need to know already is that this learning experience is structured in three parts. The first part is a general introduction to the topic of creative thinking and ideation. I see this first part as my opportunity to align you with much of my philosophical thinking and worldview on these matters, which serves as the context for the rest of the book. You may, of course, not agree with everything that I have to say in this part, but, in any case, it provides you with the opportunity to understand my point of reference.

The second part of the book is a deep-dive into the five activities and how they work, especially from neurological and psychological perspectives. This will not be conducted in the form of five distinct chapters, but rather from integrated analogies and frameworks that better enable you to see them as an integrated system. My goal has been to create something that makes it possible for you to intuitively 'see' how your mind and your brain form ideas.

The third and final part of the book takes a practitioner's point of view, aiming to help you create new strategies, activities and habits to put what you have learnt into practice. Coming back to the sports analogy, you can see the three parts of the book as chapters, explaining why we play this game, what the rules and the goals of the game are, and how we train to win. As with a coach, I can only show the game to you, I cannot do the hard (yet incredibly fun!) work involved in learning it.

Throughout this work, you will encounter two key teaching concepts that work particularly well to build an understanding around this rather fuzzy topic: the analogy, and the mental model. If you are similar to most people, you are probably quite familiar with the concept of analogies, but not as deeply acquainted with mental models. Let me just briefly introduce both of these ideas, and how they are useful.

Analogies exchange abstract concepts for things that you are already familiar with; for example, memories in your brain could be replaced with trees in a forest. Analogies make it possible for your mind to approximately process complex new information, without having to learn everything about the actual topic in question. Analogies are great when it comes to explaining abstract concepts, but less useful when you need to precisely process some specific information.

A mental model can be described as a thought-template that corresponds to some aspect of reality. Perhaps one of the most well-known mental models is Darwin's law, or natural selection. When we think about natural selection, we imagine nature rewarding organisms that adapt to change, while punishing those organisms that do not.

This is a mental model of what is actually going on, because reality is, of course, orders of magnitude more complex than this simple equation. But most of the time that does not matter, since the mental model enables us to think in a way that is approximately correct, in common with an analogy.

It is worth mentioning that mental models, especially those referred to as heuristics, are also largely responsible for keeping us trapped 'inside the box' when we try to think creatively. For example, we often say that a certain task can be performed according to 'best practice' - a mental model stipulating that there is a certain best way to do something. But how do we actually know that it is the best way? And best from which perspective?

Best practice is just one example of a mental model that reinforces intellectual barriers, the aforementioned 'box', when we are trying to form new ideas. Another very similar example would be so-called 'common sense'. Just because the majority of people do something, it does not therefore follow that it inevitably makes sense.

In summary, I want this work to be akin to a blueprint, appropriately backed by science, for people that wish to teach themselves to think 'outside the box'. Some parts of the book will be more theoretical than others, with the purpose of creating a deep understanding of how our minds work, or why many of our shared mental models are more harmful than helpful. But for the most part this book will provide you with practical tools that you can use to open your mind. Surely something that each and every one of us would like to achieve.

When you are ready, let us begin exploring *The Ideation Equation*.

Table of Contents

PART ONE
PREPARE

Is there really an Ideation Equation?

There is one premise that is absolutely central to this entire book - how do we acquire ideas? To answer that question we must perhaps first define the word 'idea'. That could in itself be the topic of an entire book, but let me keep it short and sweet.

Let us simply define the word 'idea' as 'a surprising proposition', not just in the eyes and minds of other people, but also for the person that conceived it. A result of thinking that yields an unpredictable, surprising suggestion. How do these surprises arise, and is there an *Ideation Equation* that can reliably produce them?

I used to think that there was no general recipe for generating ideas. But with more knowledge and experience,

I have come to the conclusion that besides a completely serendipitous path to novelty, which surely exists, there are many different methods, 'equations' or 'algorithms', that one can use to produce ideas.

However, ideas and ideation are often integrated in a larger context; what we usually refer to as 'innovation'. Consequently, most of the methods that can be utilised for ideation are actually broader innovation frameworks.

The Ideation Equation

The method that I call *The Ideation Equation* is special due to a few key reasons.

Firstly, and most importantly, this methodology is rooted in our neurobiology, and can therefore be traced through known human history, for literally thousands of years. This method existed long before whiteboards and sticky notes, even before books, and, most probably, even written language. Naturally, no evidence exists to tell us whether or not this is the case.

The Ideation Equation is not a full innovation framework, but a codification, a mental model if you will, of what can best be described as the 'neuro-natural' path to forming new ideas.

Secondly, some of the biggest, most revolutionary ideas in the history of mankind can be attributed to this specific ideation process, although time has probably made the stories of these moments more colourful than they actually were in reality.

Examples would be Archimedes' "Eureka!" moment in the bathtub, Newton's encounter with a falling apple, and, perhaps one of my favourites, Mendeleev's organisation of the elements in the periodic table - a story of *The Ideation Equation* at work that I will expand on later in this book.

And, thirdly, in our age of industrial efficiency, standardisation, quick hacks, and expectations of immediate and optimal results, our natural ideation circuitry is largely a forgotten and underutilised method for breakthrough thinking. But it is arguably the most powerful method to generate new and surprising propositions for radical change.

That is why I think it deserves to be called *The Ideation Equation* - capitalised to signify its supremacy over all other methods!

Other methods are, however, not without merit, and can actually be wonderfully complimentary tools - especially on the innovation journey that goes beyond conceiving an original idea. In an acknowledgment of this, I have included here a handful of other *'ideation equations'*, their key concepts, and a few comments on how they succeed in, as well as fall short of, making use of 'neuro-natural' creative thinking.

Design Thinking

The most famous of these frameworks is probably Design Thinking. As you will see in the following chapter, I am not particularly fond of the Design Thinking approach, but nonetheless I recognise that it can be used as a pathway to new ideas.

If you are somewhat familiar with this method, you will also see that it shares some core concepts with *The Ideation Equation*. So it is not that I believe that Design Thinking is all bad, just that I witness it taught and practised in conflict with how humans naturally think, way too often.

Design Thinking's core strength is that its nucleus is human-centric insights, or empathy. This focus is compatible with what I call 'taking control' of the brain's internal connecting of dots, in the process creating a dense area of knowledge for the brain to work with.

Design Thinking's biggest weakness is, in my experience, its reliance on brainstorming, and the assumption that people discover the best ideas as a collective in focused sessions of divergent and convergent thinking. This assumption has been disproven through research, precisely because it violates the neuro-natural way of conceiving ideas. (Mullen, Johnson & Salas, 1991)

I also believe that Design Thinking largely fails to accommodate for a neuro-natural, long-term preparation for ideation. It assumes that people have the knowledge necessary to perform well in the process, without any specific requirements for long-term learning habits, or the mindset of the people involved.

This lack of a long-term view on creative thinking also fails to recognise how, or rather when, our brains are naturally wired to spark ideas, which often leads to suboptimal results, in my experience, when entrusting the Design Thinking process to get the ideation job done.

Concept-Knowledge Design Theory

Another quite famous method for developing new ideas is the Concept-Knowledge Design Theory framework, or simply C-K Theory. This approach can be described as a way of exploring incremental paths of innovation, several steps ahead, and thereby conceiving breakthrough innovations that 'leapfrog' those several smaller steps. C-K Theory's strength is, in my opinion, its focus on the acquisition of new knowledge in order to conceive new ideas, which is consistent with the neuro-natural way of thinking about novelty.

On the other hand, C-K Theory can be overly academic in its approach to ideation and innovation, and because of its academic rigidity I have never seen it practised outside of the engineering and product development realms. The academic approach naturally leads to an over-reliance on analytical solutions to problems, despite the fact that one of the intentions within the framework is to accommodate for intuitive exploration of concepts that cannot be analytically derived or confirmed through the knowledge that is currently available to us.

SCAMPER, TRIZ and Systematic Inventive Thinking

I have clustered these three frameworks together in this review, because they share a common view of how ideas emerge from what exists today to what can be accomplished tomorrow, through the process of ideation. Systematic Inventive Thinking is even explicitly based on TRIZ (a Russian acronym for 'Theory of Inventive Problem Solving'). Rather than getting into the specifics, I would like to present these frameworks on the basis of their shared assumptions.

Each of these frameworks base their methods on acquiring deep knowledge about the problem that needs to be solved, which again is consistent with the neuro-natural way of conceiving relevant new ideas. From there, they take a template approach to transform that knowledge into new ideas; for example, the S in SCAMPER stands for 'Substitute', meaning that one way of innovating is to substitute a part of something to change that something into a new thing. 'Substitute' is followed by 'Combine', 'Adapt', 'Modify/Magnify/Minify', 'Put to another use' , 'Eliminate', and 'Reverse'.

This approach is said to be a method to 'think inside the box' (Boyd, D. & Goldenberg, J., 2013), which is an interesting way to conceptualise an ideation framework. It implies that all the knowledge required to innovate is encapsulated in the information acquired about the problem; all you need to do is to test a number of 'recipes' to rearrange that information. What I like about this is that it forces practitioners to investigate their thinking barriers, their 'boxes', and that is another factor consistent with a neuro-natural way of unlocking our brain's creative powers.

But that is where the similarities with *The Ideation Equation* end. In fact, the template approach is a way to actively reduce our brain's ability to make new and fascinating associations between the problem at hand, and any previous knowledge we may have that can be utilised in the ideation process.

Of these three frameworks, I find the SCAMPER model to be the most useful to accompany *The Ideation Equation*, because it is more of a learning tool than an ideation framework.

Lateral Thinking

Edward de Bono's concept of Lateral Thinking is probably one of the most influential frameworks related to creativity and ideation of the past 50 years. At its core is non-linear reasoning based on four thinking tools, each of which have features that can be loosely linked to a neuro-natural ideation process; such as random learning and associations, idea capture techniques, and the breaking down of thinking barriers.

De Bono also held the belief that creative thinking is a skill that can be learnt, which is consistent with modern research on the subject. But much of the remainder of his ideas have been challenged as pseudoscientific, or shamelessly borrowed from other academics; rebranded and presented as the fruits of his own genius.

No doubt, many of the teachings encapsulated in Lateral Thinking have had a positive impact on the world, especially when it comes to breaking out of stagnant thinking patterns, with the intention of 'thinking outside the box'. But this framework also fails to account for key neurological ideation subprocesses, most notably what is usually referred to as 'subconscious incubation' - that is, the time that passes between giving up on efforts to solve a problem, and suddenly having a 'eureka moment'.

James Webb Young's Technique for Producing Ideas

I could keep listing frameworks for ideation and creative thinking, comparing them to *The Ideation Equation*, for yet many pages, but that would probably be a waste of your time. Instead, I want to present one final method, and one of special interest!

The creative thinker and writer that deserves credit for describing the most neuro-natural ideation technique that I have encountered is James Webb Young. In 1939, his 60-page book, *A Technique for Producing Ideas* (McGraw Hill), was first published, with a second edition printed in 1965. Sounds a lot like *The Ideation Equation*, right?!

Young was a highly creative American advertising executive who had a profound idea: "the mind follows an operative technique which can be learned and controlled". His method of achieving ideation was to follow the natural tendencies of the mind, and model the creative process after those tendencies; an approach that could more or less serve as the definition of a neuro-natural ideation framework.

Young's *Technique for Producing Ideas* comprises five distinct steps:

1. Gather raw material, always and everywhere;
2. Examine all of the material related to a certain challenge;
3. Let the unconscious mind process the material, and sleep on it;
4. Capture the 'aha-moment', when you least expect it;
5. Expand the idea as needed, so that it fits the world.

The Ideation Equation also entails five distinct factors (I refrain from using 'steps'):

1. Learn about all sorts of random things;
2. Expand your thinking box;
3. Make use of your brain's innate ability to connect things;
4. Take control by marinating in a specific challenge;
5. Capture and make sense of your brain's magic.

So is this book a rip-off of Young's almost century-old classic on creativity? Not quite, even though you may find that many of his experiences and ideas are also present in my work.

The big difference between the two is that, in this book, I go much deeper into why creativity is suppressed in most people nowadays, how our brains work in relation to creativity and ideation, techniques that you can use to evolve your creative thinking, among other subjects. I would like to think of Young's book as an inspiration, and a companion, to my work.

Above all else, we know so much more about creativity and how the brain works today than we did in the 1930s, mostly thanks to modern science. But regardless of that new knowledge, it still takes time and effort to become great at ideation. But, conversely, that is really all it takes! Of course, this investment of time and effort must also be allied with the knowledge of how to employ it effectively in order to achieve optimal results.

Providing that knowledge to Daniel was my initial goal with this text; consequently, it is also what this book has been written to achieve for others. I promise you that all of the guidance you need to become a creative genius is contained within these pages!

You may consider that this is not a particularly humble thing to say as an author. But I only make this claim because I place a reasonable trust in science, and most of the ideas herein are not my own, but simply a collection of fact-based principles for how ideation works, *neuro-naturally.*

My ambition has not been to write a quasi-academic popular science book full of quotes and references to scientific studies, though. I think there are already far too many such books in the world, and they inevitably rob the reader of the opportunity to think critically about the subject at hand, due to studies making various claims, many of which are either conflicting, or poorly supported.

Even distinguished academic authors risk getting lost in the process of writing such books, including Nobel laureate Daniel Kahneman, who said in an interview with Shane Parrish:

"Some of the stuff that I really believed in when I wrote Thinking Fast and Slow, some of that evidence has been discredited. So I've had to change my mind...I believed it, and I wrote it as if it were true because the evidence suggested it. In fact, I thought that you had to accept it because that was published evidence." (The Knowledge Project #68, 2019)

Instead of following this archetypal academic pathway, I have, in general, been inspired by science to build analogies that are easy to follow and internalise. There are a few references to studies and books within these pages, but for the most part you should process the information in this text as my opinions and interpretations, rather than the absolute truth. The world, and the mind in particular, are far too complex for anyone to ever say that they "know" them. (And for the record, I think Daniel Kahneman is mostly awesome!).

Before moving on to discussing the environment for creative thinking that we currently live in, such as our shared beliefs, modern mental traps, and the effects of our schooling; I firstly wish to share the fact that there is at least one very famous mathematical equation that is directly applicable to the method I describe here: Bayes' theorem of conditional probability.

It would not make much sense if I was to explain right now why that is, so I am saving that for later in this book. But hey, nothing keeps you reading like a classic cliffhanger!

What do you believe?

So much of what we collectively believe about creativity and innovation today is based on propaganda, often with its origin in the American consulting and technology industries. There may be partial truth in broadly-hyped ideas, such as the 'fail fast' credo, but much of the supposed wisdom offered by short, tasty memes and inspiring talks are simply false, or only true in certain, narrow circumstances.

In this chapter, I seek to challenge the current status quo of the collective beliefs related to ideation, creativity, and innovation more generally. It will by no means be a complete picture of the myths, dogmas and memes that make up the veil of ignorance that keep many serious thinkers at arm's length from true knowledge about creativity and ideation.

But there is enough myth-busting to tear a good, broad rip in that veil, so that you come well prepared for the quite intense learning experience, about *The Ideation Equation* itself, that awaits you in part two of this book.

Before we begin the highly enjoyable, yet slightly uncomfortable, task of dissecting common knowledge about creativity and ideation, a word on how beliefs tend to change is in order. Consider the subtitle of this book: *How a handful of habits can make you a creative genius.* The keyword is 'habits', rather than beliefs. What you do shapes what you believe, much more than the other way around.

On the other hand, it is easier to do something different if we are able to see the flawed logic in our current behaviour. That enlightenment is what you should seek through this chapter, so that adopting new habits later on becomes a little bit easier.

The busted myth of the lonely genius, in need of (some) debusting

I cannot think of a better place to start than with the myth of the lonely genius, obviously. For centuries, the view that big ideas were reserved for lonesome thinkers, stereotypically lonely men with long beards and/or funny hats, prevailed; from Aristotle to Da Vinci through Newton, and so on.

But then, in 2007, empirical research suggested a different reality. An analysis of 19 million scientific papers and 2 million patents showed that teams had on average more than twice as many citations than solo researchers and inventors. The myth was considered busted, and blogs, books and podcasts were produced to cement this new paradigm.

Not so fast, is what I would like to add to this debate! I relish the fact that there is a clear link between more perceived value, ie. citations, and teamwork. That makes perfect sense, and that is how the majority of value is created in our society. Not through citations, obviously, but through people working together.

Regardless of this fact, though, there is a flaw in the logic of going from this study to debunking the idea of a correlation between loneliness and creative outbursts. After all, the study did not look at 20 million groundbreaking ideas.

Lonely creative geniuses were, and are to this day, seldom as lonely as we may think. Great thinkers, scientists, inventors, and artists are often surrounded by equally talented and dedicated partners and peers, not to mention all the great people that came before them, and indeed made their contributions possible. But that does not change the fact that solitude is, undeniably, correlated with the conception of groundbreaking ideas.

As I will come to by the end of this chapter, these two insights - that teams create more value than solo players, and that in solitude you may hatch the most valuable idea in your life - are not necessarily dichotomies. Just add a pinch of nuance to the myth, and they can both be true.

The myth of the starving genius

A very common innovation management idea is that creativity thrives when resources and options are restricted. You can pick up numerous books on this topic that expand on how to boost creativity, along with the emergence of new ideas in your organisation.

Such texts will advise you to restrict budget, time, expertise, and the investment of other resources as a proven method to achieving more and better innovations. Usually, this advice is backed up by an anecdote or two about how company such and such did this - thanks to the author's consultation, of course... and thrived!

Yet the broader empirical evidence tells a completely different story. The majority of the world's innovation originates from societies with an abundance of resources, not from those with the least freedom to spend, procrastinate, learn, and waste time, effort, and resources on experimentation.

People claiming such things as the above are overgeneralising to the point of the absurd, since the anecdotal evidence is completely contradictory to the naturally occurring quantitative empirical evidence. Or they are, as Nassim Nicholas Taleb would say, "fooled by randomness".

The cult of failure is failing you

Another hyped idea that you should not believe, is the common advice to "embrace failure", and all the variants thereof, such as "fail fast" and "fail forward". If you truly, deeply, and fully understand the nature of failure as a part of learning and succeeding, then my scepticism is probably not very thought-provoking for you.

But the truth is that most people these days have a very distorted view of failure and failing, due to all of the poorly-founded failure hype that has become almost meme-like in its ubiquity.

Firstly, to use failure as a tool to learn, and to push that idea on to other people, is very exclusionary. Unless, of course, the people romanticising failure have no problem with the pilot of the plane that they have boarded trying something new and failing! Or the surgeon operating on their spouse experimenting on the job! Or why not the teacher entrusted with the mission of educating their children? Such situations tend to bring the concept of failure into sharper focus.

To ideate and innovate, we must learn, and to learn we must experiment, and experiments may render unpredicted and unpredictable results. But experimentation is not failure, and it never has been.

Edison is often quoted as saying that he did not fail hundreds of times, he just accumulated knowledge about what did not work. Yet what prevails from interviews with the great innovator in which he expressed this philosophy has been the image of repeated failure, because that is how some of those *reporting* have interpreted Edison's methods.

Secondly, sticking with Edison as an example, most people do not understand that fruitful failure (if one must call it that) is not stochastic - that is having a random probability distribution - but, instead, systematic. Edison did not fail when testing hundreds of random materials to find an affordable lightbulb, but, in fact, carefully curated combinations based on all of the data that he had already gathered. He didn't repeatedly fail and then suddenly succeed; it was all part of the same process.

Whereas the modern interpretation of fast failing is almost exclusively to excuse one attempt at one idea that did not work. Startup people then usually claim that a pivot follows the failure. But data has revealed that in many such pivots the learning from the failure is not adequately factored in. If you want to learn by trial and error, you must do it in a system.

Thirdly, the idea that failure is life's natural teacher is largely a fallacy, particularly when it comes to things that do not have direct and immediate cause and effect relationships. For example, people that failed in their first marriage are no less likely to get divorced for a second time. In fact, the opposite is true! Failure seems to have taught them nothing! The same is true for startup founders. Entrepreneurs that fail with their first startup are no more likely to succeed the second time than any other person. And the list goes on.

Fourthly, the above phenomenon actually makes perfect sense. Because there are endless ways to fail, but only a few ways to succeed, and in many cases Edison's method would not work. For example, the different ways you can lose money in a business has no limits, but only a few configurations will yield profits. You cannot learn how to get rich by exploring all of the ways that you can be poor. Or find wisdom by accumulating ignorance.

Oftentimes, not even getting close to getting it right counts, because the world has infinite complexity, and being in relative proximity to the right answer doesn't necessarily lead you to the answer itself. Which leads me to the fifth and final point:

The greatest creators and innovators of known human history studied masters, not fools, and learned their most valuable lessons from successes rather than failures. Have you ever considered that the winners of new markets, household names such as Facebook, Netflix, Spotify, and so on, were the fastest to *win*?

So why do we not hear "embrace winning" or "win fast" more? Wouldn't this be more logical?! I believe that, aside from the myths associated with failure, there is also an underlying tendency - often among those with a vested interest - to tell people what they want to hear. People tend to want easy answers, so being told that failure is a positive is very seductive, actually, as it obviates them of the need to actually succeed!

Equally, it is very important to ensure that we do not stigmatise what we experience as failure, because to fail is as natural as to sneeze or break wind (which, similarity, are two things that you cannot avoid in life!). When it comes to having ideas, it is also the only thing all people on earth have in common: we all experience failure, but not everyone is fortunate to experience major success in their lives.

What I suggest that you do on your journey to becoming better at ideation, though, is to think through and redefine failure for yourself. You should not embrace failure, in my opinion, but rather reframe your expectations on outcomes. If you always hope for, or expect, success when you attempt to implement an idea, you will inevitably experience a lot of failure.

If you instead view all of your ideas as experiments, success can mean a well-executed such experiment, even if the hypothesis that you tested turns out to be false. This is the Edison way, and there is no better person to adopt from than one of the greatest ever inventors and innovators. If you adopt this approach, you may end up saying something like "I have not failed a single time", even if you have, like Edison, conducted hundreds of experiments without finding the 'right' answer, yet.

The myth of the mad genius

While Edison is on your mind, let me also bring up an old idea that many such intellectual giants are associated with - namely, mental illness. It is a widely held belief that creative genius, or even deep thinking in general, and insanity are closely related. Seneca (4 BC–65 AD), in his work *On The Tranquillity of Mind* quotes Aristotle expressing that "there is no great genius without a mixture of madness".

So it is a reasonable question to ask oneself if the development of a deeper creative thinking ability also risks causing a decline in mental health?

The answer to this question is that modern science does not support the notion that any such risk is real. There are lots of creative geniuses that do not suffer from any mental disorder, and there are lots of people with mental health issues that are no more creative than the average person.

However, there is a statistically significant correlation between bipolar disorder and having a scientific or artistic occupation. And being a close relative to a person with schizophrenia, bipolar disorder or anorexia, and ending up in a creative profession also seem to be clearly related. What the latter tells us is that any causation present in this correlation (if any) must indicate that such mental disorders may cause a *higher* creative ability, not the other way around.

Consequently, there seems to be no risk whatsoever for 'madness', as Aristotle put it, regardless of how deep the creative thinking skills are that you develop. Stay Calm and Keep Ideating!

The claims made by Design Thinking gurus

Another source of hype that I would like you to consider critically is Design Thinking, and all of its many variants. Design Thinking is sold as a panacea, allegedly enabling individuals, teams and entire companies to be creative on schedule and on point, by following a neat process.

Perhaps I am overgeneralising slightly, but it is an undeniable fact that the Design Thinking process prescribes activities that are completely incompatible with our neurological understanding of how ideation works, such as generating ideas in brainstorming sessions. (And saying "how might we?" does not solve this process-reality gap.)

I also encourage you to find research proving the general effectiveness of Design Thinking relative to other methods, or just plain free thinking. Yes, there are plenty of anecdotes, including several academic case studies, in which the subject of study oftentimes also paid for the research. But, as it happens, there are, to my knowledge, no credible meta studies or larger empirical datasets which suggest that Design Thinking is as effective as its worshippers claim.

One of the largest Design Thinking promoters in the world is the SAP organisation. Yes, the German IT company SAP. In 2005, the firm's co-founder Hasso Plattner donated $35 million to Stanford University, to fund the creation of the d.school at Stanford - Design Thinking's very own Mecca.

At courses held by the university, taken by myself, it is claimed that design-led companies outperform 'ordinary' companies, in terms of stock price, by hundreds of percent over a ten-year period. Yet, at the time of writing, SAP has not outperformed the S&P 500 over the past 10, or even 15 years. Perhaps, then, all of the companies in the S&P 500 are 'design-led'? Or could it instead be that such claims are completely unfounded?!

Design Thinking is not worthless, far from it! To focus on real problems and on real people is as good as innovation advice gets. But it is a process with many flaws, especially in its inherent assumptions about brainstorming and ideation, which goes against scientific insights about the brain and its (in)ability to break new ground in a social and energetic context. This is, of course, something we will explore much more deeply in part two of *The Ideation Equation*.

People look smart by saying "this, not that"

Coming back to the lonely genius versus value of teamwork clash: you should always be suspicious of any hype based on an either/or statement. The reality is that almost everything is better if you think about perceived dichotomies as both/and.

Here are a few examples: "Do not hire for skills, hire for attitude" accompanied with a few thousand thumbs up and back-slaps on your favourite social networking platform.

Your best option is, of course, to hire someone with both great skills and attitude.

Or: "Great companies do not sell products, they sell ideas about who you want to be". Actually, they do sell products (or services); that is how they make money! But the latter statement is nonetheless also true, and there is no inherent conflict between those two aspects of corporate success.

And my favourite: "Do not invest in great ideas, invest in great teams". Personally, I prefer to look for a promising combination, because I do not believe we must opt for one or the other.

This insight is one of the greatest takeaways of Jim Collins' book *Built to Last* (HarperCollins, 1994), in which he calls it "the tyranny of OR". Collins has received a lot of criticism for a lack of scientific rigour in his approach, mostly claiming that due to selection bias his studies of leaders and companies only reveals correlations and not causations. Assuming, for the sake of the argument, that such critique is well-founded, it ironically serves as a perfect example of how Collins is right: he can have a flawed method, AND still have a great message.

To succeed at becoming great at ideation, and truly learn *The Ideation Equation*, you must try to see through the hype and propaganda. Because virtually all the creativity and innovation myths and memes that go around have one promise in common: a shortcut to greatness. And yet, very rarely will these shortcuts yield any substantial results.

Bring this insight with you as you read the rest of this book, remember that 'AND is almost always better'. And so we will explore focused AND diffused thinking, solitude AND social influences, random exploration AND controlled ideation, and so on. The only thing you cannot have is novelty AND efficiency, but that is due to logic we will explore in part two of *The Ideation Equation*.

Do you think inside a box?

If you are like Daniel, you now have your hand raised and want to ask this author "when can I learn about *The Ideation Equation*?". "Soon, my young apprentice" I would answer, in my head. In reality I would say that the five questions that make up the chapters of part one of this book, are already contributing to the learning process.

Before we can learn the heavy stuff, we need to understand why it is that we even need to learn something that is supposed to be 'neuro-natural'. So it is time to leave the innovation-myths and hacks of the previous chapters behind, and go a bit deeper.

We often hear people refer to ideation as "thinking outside the box". You will, in fact, encounter the term, in various forms, about a hundred times throughout this book. You may, indeed, rightfully ask why I bring up another over-hyped and distorted mental model for creative thinking, immediately after making a promise to go deeper?

The answer is twofold:

Firstly, the phrase has become a management prescription that we cannot escape in any practical way, so why not try to drill down into its true meaning and make it useful?

Secondly, the original research that led to the minting of the think outside the box mantra actually reveals a deep and fundamental truth about our thinking to which we should pay constant attention.

It is not entirely clear from where the idea that there is a box around our thinking originated. But clearly, the American psychologist J.P. Guilford played an important part in 'formalising' this idea. He designed experiments in the 1960s and 1970s, in which participants were tasked to draw lines on a piece of paper, with the objective being to *connect the dots* organised in a square pattern.

"Connect the dots by drawing 4 straight lines, without lifting the pen"

To solve this puzzle, it is necessary to draw the lines beyond the square area where the dots are neatly organised. Initially, none of the participants in the study solved the puzzle, but after asking Guilford if it was okay to draw "outside the box" (ie. the 'invisible square' containing the dots), 20% of the participants solved it.

Most people perceive a 'box' that they are limited to when trying to solve this problem

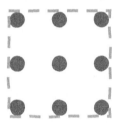

To solve the problem one must draw (or think) outside this imaginary box

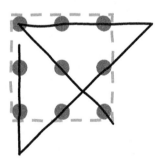

And so, within a few years of publication of these findings, the most notorious metaphor for creative thinking was born; the ability to think outside the box. (Originally, the saying was to think outside the *dots*). Since then, the term has been used and abused in all imaginable and unimaginable ways, and there are countless books, articles and courses trying to teach outside-the-box thinking.

But almost every resource that I have encountered is, in my opinion, missing the key point that Guilford unearthed: we are all mentally trapped inside boxes, not only *cognitively*, but, in fact, for *a variety* of reasons. What I think those interpretations of Guilford's study gets wrong is the narrow focus on cognitive bias; ie. that in order to solve the puzzle you have to 'unsee' the box around the dots and 'creatively' venture out into the white space.

The insight that our cognition is constantly creating unreal boundaries, to which we nonetheless adhere, is not wrong. But just as revealing, if not more so, is the fact that people politely asked if they were allowed to draw outside of the imaginary box. That fear of not conforming with expectations is a factor just as limiting to free thought as any bias related to our cognition. We will address this concept, and some of the reasons that I believe it is perpetuated, as the book unfolds.

In two later studies, other academics (Burnham C., Davis K., Alba J., and Weisberg R.) repeated Guilford's experiment, but altered it by telling participants that they were *required* to draw outside of the imaginary box to solve the puzzle. In these studies still only 25% managed to find a solution.

This research is often presented as counter-evidence to Guilford's findings; ie. that telling people to think outside the box has no significant effect on creative problem-solving capabilities, only a statistically insignificant 5%.

I beg to differ! What these studies collectively illustrate is that the 'box' is a contextual mental state, in which intellectual limitations are compounded. The studies to solve the nine-dot puzzle are just very simple examples in which two such limitations are exposed; ie. the cognitive bias of seeing a square around the dots, that does not exist, and the fear of looking like an idiot by breaking some untold, but seemingly obvious, rule. What is not exposed in the studies are the barriers to creative thinking that make up the remaining 75% of failure to solve the puzzle.

The box is real, even if the term is a bit silly. Every situation we encounter, every second of our lives, is intellectually pinned down in a myriad of different ways. We are most aware of these barriers as 'cognitive filters'; effectively, sorting out and discarding the vast majority of actual impressions that reach us. But how we think in every situation is equally defined and limited by our experiences, beliefs, values, attitudes, manners, expectations, and feelings, as well as our physiology, awareness, and chemistry; in fact, the list goes on even beyond these factors.

What Guilford's research showed was that removing

just one such barrier (the fear of wrongdoing) can have a significantly positive effect on intellectual performance and output. But what subsequent research demonstrated was that simply telling people that they need to think outside the box in order to perform has a negligible impact on intellectual ability.

But the implication of that is not that there is no box, as some suggest. Rather, it is not so simple to break through the barriers that constrain us within this box as thinkers, as to simply wish for it to go away. We need to apply better strategies than that in order to think outside the box.

So what do I suggest that one should do in order to get outside of the box?

Firstly, always acknowledge that the box is there in every situation. It is a well-known and proven fact that even the brightest thinkers in the world have to contend with their own thinking barriers.

Secondly, acknowledge that there are systemic forces in your head that act as the foundation of the limitation of your thinking and creativity. The most prevalent and harmful of these forces is the fear of looking like an idiot. If you are like most people, fear is the ceiling of your mental box in almost every situation. So find a way to ditch it. (Actually, I will give you several pieces of advice throughout this book for how to deal with fear, but you may want and need to go beyond what I have to offer.)

Thirdly, acknowledge that what appears super-creative to you is merely routine to someone else, simply because of your different levels of relevant experience, skills, and knowledge. All of these acquired intellectual assets can be double-edged swords, though, potentially creating as many new barriers to free thinking as they alleviate.

But, generally, more experiences, skills and knowledge provide more escape routes from boxed thinking. A great way to get unstuck in a situation where you need to creatively solve a hard problem is to learn more about the problem itself. Just avoid making a hammer out of your learnings, and treating everything else like a nail.

Fourthly, make a habit out of studying your own boxes, and look for limiting assumptions that you can flip 180-degrees to instantly get outside the box in which you are currently stuck. Common opportunities to perform this kind of trick lay in questioning our beliefs about other people, and how the world works at large; for example, if you are stuck when trying to solve a problem, partly because you believe that people hate standing in line, what solutions would be possible if they actually loved queueing? Or if gravity is limiting your thinking, how would you solve the same problem that you're grappling with in space?

Fifthly, routinely try to think like someone else; ie. swap your box for some other person's box, as you imagine it. How would Charlie Munger think about the situation at hand? Or your child? Or a grandparent? Or why not Jesus, or Buddha? What intellectual barriers would they encounter?

It is important, though, not to fall into the trap of thinking that however you imagine your role-model reasoning is automatically going to be brilliant. After all, you are not Charlie Munger (unless you actually are Charlie Munger?) or Jesus (you are definitely not Jesus). But this exercise is a great way of exposing the constituents of your own mental cage. Only when you see it, can you consciously break it.

We must, however, acknowledge that the box is a lifesaver in almost every situation! If we did not have thought barriers constantly guarding our intellectual activities, we would be completely exhausted within an hour of getting out of bed in the morning. What are all possible ways of getting dressed? Why do we even wear clothes? Should I crawl, walk, jump, or perhaps swim to the kitchen? Why drink coffee in the morning? And what should I put in my coffee? Milk seems just way too much inside the box... In summary, these reflections should make it clear that even the greatest outside the box thinkers are still mostly inside the box, but they know when to revolt, and give their brains the freedom to flourish.

One interesting way to look at the box is to reverse the mental model of it. That is, instead of imagining a small box inside a large thinking space, imagine the box being as large as possible, filling up the entirety of your mind. Similarly, what determines the extremities of your ability to think?

One answer could be that the very fabric that enables us to think is the same stuff that ultimately limits us. Some studies suggest that 25% of people think only in words, which illustrates that language is, in itself, a barrier. Another

30% think exclusively in images, which impose another kind of limitation. The rest of us think in both words and images, which raises the question of whether we get a combination of the best or the worst of these two boxes?

As the very real, yet invisible, existence of the box around our thinking becomes clear to us, the natural and profound reaction is to seek a place to start peeking over its edges. You may feel that the general advice that I provide above is not tangible enough, or not applicable for your way of thinking. Rest assured, I will give much more specific instructions, coupled with examples related to learning and ideation that you should be able to recognise, in just a few chapters.

Did school really ruin your creativity?

It is a fairly widespread belief that schools, at least the regular Western kind, are robbing kids of their creativity. To have such a belief you must also, for the sake of simple logic, believe that mainstream schools are capable of fundamentally altering how our brains function, including inhibiting already established functions in children, such as creativity and imagination.

Personally, I do not think either is true. Schools do not kill creativity, and they are not powerful enough to fundamentally change our brains, they mostly just fill it with stuff. But, no doubt about it, something happens during schooling that appears to bring most childish creativity and imagination to a halt, or at least reduce them to much lower levels. Is that something that is simply correlated with the period in which we go to school, or is there a causal connection?

I do not have a conclusive answer to this question, but my suspicion is that creative thinking is starved rather than killed in school, by the process of schooling itself. Children's creativity is slowly forced into hibernation, rather than resting in peace forever, waiting inside our minds for its moment to unfurl.

You should not only consider the common narrative about the education system's damaging effect on creativity here, but thoroughly examine your self-beliefs and doubts. In the previous chapter about beliefs, we focused on the external world, hypes and hacks that give us falsehoods about how the world works. For this and the following chapter, you should pay attention to what beliefs about your internal world which my thought-provocations bring to light. If all these shared beliefs about creativity and innovation are flawed, could it also be that your limiting self-beliefs are unfounded?

I asked Daniel to engage in this kind of self-reflection, and his answer may serve as a good example:

"For a very long time, my core belief about creative thinking was that it is an inborn talent, and that there was little I could do to improve my ability to be creative. In my mind, imagination and creativity were not learned skills; they were either something that you were blessed with, or not.

This flawed belief prevented me from developing my creative faculties for years; since I didn't think that cultivating a more creative mind was possible, I never attempted to do so.

Another belief that held me back was that my edge

wasn't my creative thinking skills. Even though I never had any reason to doubt my aptitude for creativity, it just felt more like me to be logical, rational, and efficiency-oriented in my approach to thinking. Subconsciously, I assumed that the focused mindset could help me achieve the same level of success as creative thinking, with less risk of failure.

But what I realised at Eicorn, and from working with Linus in particular, is that leaning on only one thinking style is like "being a one-legged man in an ass-kicking contest", as Charlie Munger would say. Rather than having to choose between rationality and creativity, I have come to realise that these two qualities are complementary.

Fast forward to today; creativity and imagination are now becoming integrated parts of my thinking and problem-solving routines, while daily improvement through creative habits have become second nature."

Coming back to the subject of school's suppressing effect on creative thinking, a key question to ask is: how does this occur, in terms of what mechanism it is that results in this outcome?

To answer this question, let us once again consider the subtitle of this book; or why not imagine an entire, corresponding, title to illustrate what happens in school. *The Education Equation - how a handful of habits can make you an uncreative worker.* Or, to be fair, if this was a real title it would probably not use the word 'uncreative', but something like 'productive', 'efficient', or perhaps 'attractive'.

The point I wish to make, though, is not about the differences between *The Ideation Equation - How a handful of habits can make you a creative genius,* and *The Education Equation - how a handful of habits can make you an uncreative worker,* but what is common. As in the previous example, I want to direct your attention to the word 'habits'. This book is designed to help you change your mind through the adoption of habits, things you start doing routinely that soon will influence what you believe, how you think, and ultimately who you are.

Would it be too far-fetched to say that habits are a form of programming? This is debatable, but I would argue that habits can become a form of positive programming, if designed appropriately, or even inappropriately in some circumstances.

The diminishing of creative powers which we are discussing, takes place in school through the use of behaviour that programs our thinking towards a certain default mode; a kind of foundational heuristic. Western society decided a long time ago that what it wanted out of schooling was predictability and conformity.

Basically, what early school reformists desired was to create a kind of intellectual monoculture - a term that you will learn more about in part two of this book. They did this to create efficiency; the main force driving industrialisation forward. Ironically, those who were less susceptible to intellectual standardisation were the ones that ultimately created the innovations that benefitted from an intellectually efficient and conformist workforce.

How this particular mental programming works is ridiculously simple, and it leads to a fundamental, deep belief that is so pervasive in our thought process as adults that we cannot see it. From an early age, we are taught that every question has one correct, or optimal, answer.

Before children start school there is no such deeply-rooted belief gatekeeping their thinking. If you tell a young enough child that two plus two can be four, or cheese, or the name of a rare type of seahorse, or how dogs see cats, or seven, they would be amazed, but not necessarily confused.

Adults, on the other hand, would be guided by this foundational heuristic to say that only *one* answer is correct. We adults like to think that this instinct arises because we know better, but I would argue that it is because we are programmed to look for singular, optimal answers to every question. In academic terms, this is known as a 'representativeness heuristic', but in my view it would make more sense to simply refer to it as a 'blueprint heuristic'.

I stated above that the process to accomplish this is extremely simple. Here is how it works: on the first day of school, your teacher establishes a pattern. They ask you "what is your name, dear?", a question for which you have the correct answer. "What is one plus one?". "How do you spell 'apple'?". On that first day alone, you probably encountered this thought pattern at least ten times.

During the first year, it will be repeated thousands of times, and before you are through school hundreds of thousands, perhaps even millions of times. By the time that you complete your schooling, this mode of thought has become your default behaviour; a blueprint, to seek singular, optimal and (perhaps most importantly) already established external answers to any and all questions. A way of expressing this is to say that you seek answers by the means of external analysis.

Now, ask yourself this: "how exposed was I to other essential thought patterns in school?". For example "what could this apple do?". Well, it could feed you, or be a projectile, or you could give it a face and have long philosophical conversations with it, or you could take a bite and then make a logo out of it, or you could collect billions of apples and fill a stadium with them (for no particular reason). Which answer is optimal, and the right one?

This example is only one that exposes a thinking pattern that deviates from the 'blueprint heuristic' that questions have one optimal external answer, but there are many more such models. What these non-conformist thinking styles do, or at least some of them, is to nurture your creativity and imagination, so that you can conceive an internal answer; ie. an idea for how to do something - how to solve a problem or create an opportunity that cannot be externally verified through analysis.

A way of expressing this type of thinking is to say that you seek an answer by means of internal exploration. Because it comes from inside your head. How many such ideas did school ask of you? How many such answers did it accept as 'correct'? How many times was the process required to generate these answers encouraged, or even tolerated? Many respondents to these questions would inevitably find themselves answering "zero" or "never"!

So do not beat yourself up for not being as creative as you wish you were, or as you see others being. People are born with somewhat different intellectual dispositions for these different types of thinking. But, even more than that, I believe that we have varying internal and external prerequisites that determine the extent to which we can be completely reprogrammed into efficient single-right-answer type thinkers.

I do not believe, however, that the starving of creativity and imagination was an intended consequence of the modern Western schooling system when it was established. I am no expert, but as I have understood historical accounts of those early reforms, they sought to create higher base rates of general knowledge that would be useful for the growing gains of standardised work. Or, in less words, the education of a capable workforce to drive industrialisation forward. Creativity was not impeding this mission as such, it was simply not prioritised, or even embraced, as part of the overall system.

Since these early days, though, the standard curriculum has grown into a thinking process reprogramming activity (and, to be fair, useful stuffing too) that we engage in for at least a full decade of our lives.

What is now missing in school is a sound balance between 'correct' and 'creative' thinking. For most people, the balance between external and internal answers requested by teachers during their school-years is probably at least 1,000 to 1. For some children, though, this balance is tilted back in the direction of creative thinking through interactions outside of the regular curriculum.

It has been suggested that there is broad empirical evidence that this hypothesis may be true. In the 1980s and 90s Sweden in which I grew up, we had a massive free public music school, where children would play instruments from a very young age. We were fortunate in that there was a wide variety of instruments available; we could pretty much play whatever we wanted.

As a consequence of this, hundreds of thousands of kids attended the public music schools (and still do) without any other intention from the state than to "provide an opportunity to develop an instrument or singing skill regardless of economic, cultural or social background".

Since this intention was so free of 'expected productive outcome', the music schooling soon became mostly jamming, a lot of improvisation, experimenting with numerous different instruments, and, for many, joining a band or choir.

It is hard to support what I am now about to hypothesise with evidence, but I believe it to be true: a couple of decades after the big scale-up of public music schools, which happened in the 1980s, Sweden became one of the most innovative countries in the world - at the time of writing ranked number two after Switzerland, according to the Global Innovation Index.

This is related to public music schools providing balance to the thinking development process of children, nurturing their creativity and imaginative capabilities in parallel with the intellectual standardisation efforts of regular schools. Sweden is also the world's third-largest music exporter, after the USA and the UK.

There is also a commonly used metaphor for creative ability which fits well with this reasoning - that creativity is like a muscle. If you do not use it, your creative power will diminish. If you do use it, then it will remain functional. If you challenge that muscle, it will grow and increase your ability. I believe this is true, and that it can serve as a great and important analogy if put into a somewhat larger context.

Imagine that analytical thinking is also a muscle, or rather all of the muscles, within one of your arms. Creative thinking is also part of this analogy... you guessed it, it's all of the muscles on your other arm. Can you imagine this? If thinking skills were this visual to us, curricula in ordinary Western schools would not be designed the way that they are, because everyone would realise that we train only one side of our childrens' bodies.

For over ten years, children and young adults are incentivised to build their efficient, analytical, external correct answer arm, while being simultaneously discouraged to use their creative, internal exploration arms. In fact, they are sometimes even punished and downgraded for using this forbidden arm!

Here is why this serves as a great analogy: your, by now, super-strong, analytical arm does not in any way inhibit your potential or ability to train your creative arm. The two ways of thinking are largely independent! Being a super-strong analytical thinker does not inherently lower your potential to be just as strong with your creative arm.

But you do probably need to focus your attention and training on that creative arm, and grow it for a while, before you believe this to be true. That includes having the discipline to refuse to allow the analytical arm to do all of the work as soon as things start to get heavy. That is why establishing habits, which act as rules for how to behave, is so effective for self-change.

Limiting some of the lazy use of the single-optimal-answer 'blueprint heuristic' that you have developed in school, and most likely also at work - ie. your analytical arm - can account for one important part of the secret to becoming great at thinking outside the box. This process enables you to complement analytical thinking with a more creative thinking style, and exercise that creativity strongly enough that you can choose in the future which arm you would like to use at any given moment.

This can be considered 'thinking ambidexterity' - the ability to be equally capable of finding answers externally through analysis, as well as internally through curiosity and exploration. Once you have developed these two very separate forms of thinking, you will find that, rather than impeding one another, they are entirely complementary.

Are you eager to learn?

You have almost completed the orientation part of this book, and it will soon be time to dive into the exploration of *The Ideation Equation* in part two. But first, you should ask yourself if you are totally excited and endlessly eager to learn this very special ideation technique?!

Or, if there is, perhaps, a tiny voice somewhere in your head, telling you with just a whisper that it will be a futile effort? We all have egos, and by that I do not mean that we are being egoistic, but there is a kind of autonomous internal 'self' that is always trying to defend the status quo.

Throughout this chapter, we are going to ensure that this potential hurdle for learning and changing shuts up! And the first thing to do in achieving this outcome is to start thinking about how much fun you are going to have learning this stuff, and how much fun you are then going to have with your new ideas! I just realised that the biggest problem with this book so far, is that it sounds way too serious!

Now, switch from seriousness to excitement, and do not read on until you are smiling!

I cannot see you, but I trust you. And wearing that beautiful smile, you should already feel a bit more confident about the learning adventure ahead of you. Am I right? If your answer is 'yes', which I am going to presume it is, how can that be? To answer this question, let me begin by making two important distinctions.

Firstly, there is the perception of things, including change, which may or may not align with reality.

Secondly, there is reality, and actual change that on many occasions may not impact on anyone's perception, including yours. It's important to understand these contrasting positions, and acknowledge that, in this sense, perception and reality are not the same thing.

For example, you may achieve real change in your ability to think outside the box, but your colleagues may not perceive this due to how your work environment and culture functions. Another example could be that you plant the seed, a 'dot', for a glorious future idea in your head, but presently you have no perception of that future glory. The change has occurred, in reality, but there is no experience, no perception, of it.

Are you still smiling?

This relationship between reality and perception, and

the occasional disconnect between them, is important to keep in mind as you embark on your journey to learn and change, for several reasons. Above all else, perception puts so much pressure on our thinking barriers that there are many occasions on which we change reality to match that perception, rather than the other way around. Have you ever heard someone say "that person believes their own lies"?

Self-deception of this kind happens to all of us from time-to-time, mostly because we think we are more handsome, smarter, stronger, better, and so on, than we actually are. You have probably also heard the saying "fake it until you make it", which is a version of the same mental process. Since there is very compelling evidence that this type of internal and external deception works in many situations, there is even a common psychotherapy method that is referred to as to 'act as if'.

On your journey to becoming more creative, you also wish to be perceived as more creative, and therefore you should start *acting as if* you already are more creative. Just exchange 'creative' for the word 'social' in the sentence above, and you should see intuitively why this act as if behaviour is important.

That smile that is still on your face (right?), it changed your perception, perhaps just a little, but still some, of your own ability to confront the task ahead of you. But did reality change? No, it did not, though by acting as if you are already laughing on the other side of this learning journey, you are doing yourself a huge favour. Because now, with excitement and determination in your body, you are able to change reality to match that perception!

A fundamental difference with developing your creative thinking, compared with many other skills that you can add to your repertoire, is that success almost certainly means changing a bit of you as a person. Although possible, it is unlikely that learning to think in terms of macroeconomics, quantum-mechanics, or bio-engineering will have the same profound effect on your personality.

Of course, you should expect the net effect of this change to be overwhelmingly positive, even if there will be ups and downs, as with any change. When I reflect on who I am, and who I am constantly, actively, becoming, my creative side is right up there with traits such as 'loving', 'striving', and 'fully living'. For me, practising *The Ideation Equation* is a matter of making sure that I am happy and motivated to make the most of my life.

Finally, on the topic of achieving change towards more creative thinking, and how you prepare for it, I want to advise you to avoid changing *superficially*. What I mean by that is that you may get caught up in the notion that creative thinking is somehow connected to having a wild hairstyle, wearing different coloured socks, or funny t-shirts, and other externalised expressions of nonconformity, instead of your regular white collar shirt or blouse.

You may find this remark ridiculous, but it is actually not

even uncommon to see this kind of behaviour when people, for example, are promoted to an innovation role in their organisation, or move to Berlin.

To change your appearance in this manner, or to decorate your desk with pink flamingos, is not to act as if, but, instead, merely to put on a show. It is a bit like people (guys really) swagging up in tights full of logos (quasi-sponsors) to commute the seven kilometres to work on their new all-carbon race bike. (That image should bring your smile right back!).

The only time you get away with looking and acting like a cliché, at least in my opinion, is if you have always looked and behaved like one. You should, of course, wear whatever you choose, and act in any way that you want; that is none of my business, or anyone else's business for that matter. Just try not to get distracted by 'superficial creativity'. Remember that it is always *your mind* that you need to work with.

With all of these insights fresh in your head, with excitement and enthusiasm so strong we can smell them in the air, let us dive into part two of this book: Exploring creative thinking!

PART TWO
EXPLORE

Introduction to part two

How can we better understand ideation from a neurological point of view? Most of this part of the book is dedicated to answering this question, as conclusively as possible, yet from, and for, a layman's perspective. Studying the 'eureka moment' has turned out to be difficult for scientists. It is not as if they can put research subjects inside an fMRI scanner, and tell them to come up with a groundbreaking idea! (Well, they can, but it probably would not work).

Instead, scientists have mostly focused their efforts on documenting the state of mind that research subjects have been in when good ideas have come to them. From this point, these states of mind have then been studied.

There is also research that has examined the brain, during the moments when important pieces of the ideation puzzle have been presented to research subjects, such as inspiration, or the presentation of other peoples' novel ideas. Since all mammals have mimicking behaviour driven by something known as 'mirror neurons' - which also underpins the execution of intellectual tasks - it is possible to observe how the brain reacts to such stimuli, and hypothesise that similar activity was responsible for producing these puzzle-pieces in the first place.

It should be said that the neuroscience field, with regard to understanding creativity and many other mental abilities, is still in its infancy. Regardless, the volume of articles and books on the topic, and the pace at which new findings are published, is quite intimidating and humbling.

I should also say that neuroscience naturally slides over into psychology, and from psychology into social science, and from there to other concepts of interest. This makes the total volume of facts-based accounts of creative thinking mind-bogglingly large!

Joseph Campbell famously stated that "people forget facts, but they remember stories". The facts in this case would be those scientific descriptions of how neurons and synapses, the brain's hemispheres, various neural networks, and anatomy in general, its many signal substances and corresponding mental states, and so on, work relative to ideation and creativity. I have tried, as often as possible, to let these facts inspire stories in the form of analogies. I'm hopeful that by doing this they are, indeed, easier to relate to and internalise than pure facts.

In this book, and in this second part in particular, my ambition is to expand your understanding of how your brain and thinking works, from a creative practitioner's perspective. What I mean by that is that I have not tried from the scientific perspective to describe what we know about creative thinking, but, rather, I have examined some of the relevant science from a creative thinker's point-of-view.

Piece by piece, you will see *The Ideation Equation* come together throughout the following chapters, albeit in a fairly abstract form. Only towards the middle of the book will I describe the process in a more condensed and conceptualised fashion. The reason for this is that I want to help you establish a wide and flexible thinking box around the entire topic of creative thinking, before you consider how ideation works in a more simplistic way.

Too simple too soon risks getting you stuck in a false sense of understanding regarding the bigger picture - a bias that would save your brain a lot of energy, but may simultaneously prevent you from exploring the most intricate peculiarities of your creative thinking process.

Trees in a forest

An important step on your journey to more creative thinking is to better understand how your mind *and* your brain works. This is because much of the rituals and social norms in our society were formed long before we had even the most basic scientific understanding of anything related to these things. (We are, in fact, still just scratching the surface even today). So you are largely 'programmed' to do things without considering how to use as much of your biological supercomputer as possible.

Note that I am writing "your mind *and* your brain" above, as two different entities. The mind is the mental model that we use to describe everything that goes on inside our heads, in terms of thoughts, memories, feelings, consciousness, and so on. The brain is both the physical manifestation of the mind, which is of less importance here, and its operator. You can think of your mind as a machine, and the brain as the machinist, or your mind can be a garden, and your brain the gardener.

For reasons that will become clear later in this chapter, I have constructed an analogy where your mind is a forest and your brain is the forest caretaker - the ranger. A lot of interesting things go on in the forest, above and below the forest floor, but we are going to focus on the trees. In this analogy, trees are memories.

There are some very big trees that will never fall, or be outgrown by other trees, at least not as long as the ranger is healthy. These are memories that are bundled with strong emotions, such as your wedding day, when your child was born, or when your dog died. We will not focus on those memories here, but I want you to start imagining your inner forest with a few big trees and millions of smaller ones.

What we will focus on here are the millions of smaller trees. If the big trees represent significant and emotional events during your life, the small trees simply represent examples of more mundane information.

Look over there: a tree in which you can find the memory of how to fold a paper plane! And there: another tree preserving your memory of how to write VLOOKUP formulas in Microsoft Excel. How exciting!

Those trees do not only represent how-to memories, though, but also what things look like, how they smell, taste and feel (touch), and, of course, how they make you feel. Basically, everything you learn becomes a new tree in the forest, as well as every thought that the ranger considers worth preserving also remains in your forest as a tree of its own.

There is one characteristic above all others that we need to understand and remember when it comes to our forest rangers, or brains. They are lazy! Let us not judge them too harshly, though. There are good reasons for them to be lazy. The forest is vast (it seems, in fact, that it can grow indefinitely), and it takes an enormous amount of energy to run around and keep the trees organised in the most functional and efficient way.

Consequently, rangers try to plant trees to which you need frequent access as close to their cabins as possible, and whenever we ask them open questions, those lazy bastards try to direct us to trees that are as near as possible. (In other words, they put us inside a 'box', sound familiar?!)

A good example of this as-near-as-possible behaviour is what we call heuristics - mental shortcuts that preserve energy, but may not give optimal answers. Most of the time, heuristics work pretty well, but when it comes to creative thinking they can be your worst enemy! Let me give you a simple example:

Imagine that when you were 15 years-old, a person with a very peculiar accent made a fool out of you in school. This became a semi-large tree, nurtured and anchored by negative emotions, that the ranger kept in his 'may-come-in-handy' patch, not far from the cabin. Now you are 40, and in a meeting with a startup founder that proposes a unique collaboration with your firm. The founder has the same peculiar accent. Can you guess the outcome?

The ranger's first attempt to answer the open question that you are now asking yourself - "is this collaboration a good idea?" - will likely apply to something known as the 'contamination heuristic'. The ranger will try to answer your question subconsciously (because that's a lot less work than to run all of the way up your consciousness ladder) with: "we know that bloody accent, don't we!?", and bombard you with the feeling of anger and distrust that's associated with that 25-year-old flourishing tree behind the ranger's cabin. The consequence is that you tell the founder that your firm is not interested, and miss what could have been the opportunity of your career.

Rarely do we spot thinking errors such as this one. Yet such heuristics, as well as much more mundane thinking patterns than the example given above, are what makes up most of the intellectual barriers to thinking outside the box. For the ranger, though, it is a double win!

Firstly, it only took a short walk out to this easy-to-find tree in the may-come-in-handy patch behind the cabin.

Secondly, since you accepted this simple answer, no more trees need to be planted today. The ranger effectively shut down what would certainly have become a big and tiresome learning effort, with a lot of new trees to plant as part of this process.

If you read this and feel a need to argue against it... if you think "I am not like that!"... let me just say that we *all* are. I am no better, and this lazy feature of our brains is one that we need, as discussed previously. For most scenarios, the ranger's laziness serves us well.

Most of the time, we want to stay inside the box with our thoughts and decisions, otherwise even the simplest decision would require an inordinate amount of effort, and life would become logistically impossible. But to venture outside the box intellectually, we need to employ strategies to override the ranger's laziness.

Before we examine those strategies, I want you to think about what kind of forest you have in your head, and what type you think is optimal for coming up with big ideas. If you are a specialist of some sort, have one or two long-term hobbies, and do not read much random stuff, your forest probably resembles what biologists call a 'monoculture'.

You may have a very big and useful forest, featuring a lot of experience as an expert, but the trees will all more or less resemble one another. This is what a typical cultivated commercial forest looks like. It is impressive, valuable, resilient, beautiful in many ways, but monotone.

Monoculture

If you, on the other hand, are a jack of all trades, someone that likes to try everything at least once, and learn as much as possible about anything and everything before you die, your forest is probably very messy. You do not have any special expertise or skill, but, on the other hand, nobody can beat you at trying something for the first time.

Your forest is the opposite of a monoculture; it is a 'polyculture'. You may have a very big forest, but it is not easy to take a walk around in there without getting lost or stuck. This is what it is like to spend time in a tropical rainforest.

This illuminating comparison between a cultivated commercial forest and a wild rainforest is why I used the forest as an analogy to represent the mind. Because we can, from this perspective, look at nature and intuitively draw a parallel to our analogy of the mind. What is innovation in nature? I would like to think that it is diversity. Evolution at work, creating as many useful solutions for life as possible.

Polyculture

Where is this most likely to happen in nature? You guessed it - in a rainforest! Conversely, well-kept, cultivated forests score relatively low on the biodiversity scale. If you seed and nurture an inner forest of great diversity, with many very different trees, that forest will be capable of serving you with an equally great diversity of new ideas! Note that here I am using the phrase 'capable of', rather than 'destined to'.

In other words, if you want to become an outside-the-box thinker, a very good strategy is to increase the probability of remarkable things happening in the forest. The bigger the rainforest that you can plant and nurture in your head, the better the chances that you will come up with many wonderful and unconventional ideas in the future.

If you already have a monoculture up there, that is not a problem! Our rangers may be lazy, but they are such amazing forest keepers that they can handle a mix of mono and polycultures. In fact, I would argue that the combination of a vast rainforest and a couple of different monocultures, such as expert areas of knowledge, is the ultimate setup for great outside-the-box thinking.

Much empirical evidence, albeit sometimes anecdotal in nature, would suggest that this may indeed be the case. Elon Musk, for example, perhaps one of the most creative yet practical thinkers of our time, fits this description well. (Regardless of anyone's opinion of him, and his many questionable decisions). As a child, he planted an enormous rainforest in his mind by reading the *Encyclopaedia*

Britannica, rather than watching TV. As an adult, he continues to read and learn out of pure curiosity, and has established multiple fields of expertise that he combines with his rich understanding of how the world works.

Another great example is Hedy Lamarr, although she appears to have had a completely different strategy than Musk. Lamarr was an Austrian-American actress and inventor, born in 1914, who used impressions and inspiration from the arts and nature to conceive groundbreaking ideas in science. She helped aviation pioneer Howard Hughes design faster aeroplanes, and she improved the way that traffic lights work.

But, perhaps most famously, inspired by composer George Antheil's unpredictable avant-garde piano compositions, she co-invented what today is known as frequency-hopping, which is an essential principle in GPS, CDMA, WiFi, and Bluetooth technologies. You can find Lamarr's name on a star on the Hollywood Walk of Fame, as well as in the Inventors Hall of Fame.

Let us get back to the forest because we are not quite done there yet. The first major point of the forest analogy should now be clear - the first thing to do on your journey to becoming better at outside-the-box thinking is to increase the probability of naturally occurring innovations; i.e. the evolution of diverse new species in the rainforest. You can accomplish this by varying your learning as much as possible, effectively planting a little bit of everything.

But now let us focus once more on the ranger. Apart from being inherently lazy, rangers have two more behaviours that we need to understand in depth to get better at using our brains optimally to think outside-the-box. In neuroscience terms, these two behaviours can be referred to as 'focused thinking' and 'diffused thinking', and we are notoriously bad at using them to our advantage. Let us start with exploring focused thinking because that will likely be most familiar to you.

It is easy to understand what the ranger is doing when in focused thinking mode, since we are all so familiar with the concept of being focused. Basically, we have a plan when we focus, and we ask the ranger to execute on that plan. It could be to solve a logical problem, such as six plus four, or to take care of new information arriving through our senses, as you are doing right now by reading this book. The ranger has created specific paths in the forest to efficiently deal with focused problem-solving, and has a clear patch of land just next to the cabin where new trees can be planted directly as they arrive.

Running around in focused mode, the ranger is not very interested in trying something new and unexpected, something outside the box. Rather, it is trying to execute on your plan as efficiently (lazily) as possible, and to make the management of newly arrived trees as simple as possible, knowing that it must deal with those again later.

Your best use of a focused ranger is either to work on a problem where you need more structure, logic and tangible answers, or to give it as many different and strange new trees as possible, which it will then feel obliged to deal with.

It is not as easy to understand the diffused mode of thinking, because it is not as intuitive as focused mode, and most people do not use diffused thinking in the same deliberate way. Let me describe it like this: when you put the ranger in focused mode you have a plan, which means that it is being supervised; when you put the ranger (or it puts itself) in diffused mode, you do not have a plan, which means it is unsupervised.

This naturally also means that it is harder to observe, and therefore our understanding of rangers doing diffused work is limited. But for the creative thinker, the diffused mode is key!

This is how I imagine the ranger when it gets deeply into the diffused mode of thinking. The first thing it does is to praise its Gods and Goddesses for providing a break from the annoying human being that controls it with plans and supervision most of the time. It is just so exhausting...

But as the ranger takes control, it starts to experience the beauty, strangeness and mystery of the forest surrounding it in all directions. Its awakened curiosity drives the ranger to take a closer look at the most recently planted trees close to the cabin, those that it quickly planted as new memories which were to be dealt with later. It decides that later is now, so it picks one up, and starts to experience it more intimately.

If the new tree is one akin to the millions planted in the monoculture part of the forest, the ranger does not give it much more thought, instead wandering off to the monoculture to permanently plant it there with the other similar trees. Oftentimes, the ranger also decides to completely discard new trees, that is, to forget things. You may, for example, remember the last time you took a shower, but not necessarily the time before that, or before that, and so on.

But if the new tree it picks up is of a new variety, or just not something that the ranger immediately recognises, it will start to do something very interesting. As the ranger explores the new mystical tree, it will simultaneously wander off into the forest. It will try to match the tree with others, so that it can decide where in the forest the new tree will find optimal conditions to become rooted, grow, and thrive. On its diffused random walk of exploration, the ranger will try to match any specificity of the new tree with the features of the trees that it encounters in the forest.

This process is more or less completely subconscious, but sometimes it becomes available to our consciousness in various forms. If you have experienced daydreaming that is not focused on some particular desire or plan, but is instead just rather random and strange, then you have witnessed the ranger on one of its diffused tree-matching walks in the forest.

Or if you have experienced a completely unexpected eureka moment in the shower, or just before falling asleep, then you have also reaped the benefits of diffused thinking flowing over into the conscious domain. Training yourself to do this type of thing more often is also one of the key strategies to become really good at thinking outside of the box, and we will explore this later in the book.

I used the word 'flowing' in the previous paragraph, which may sound familiar to you within the context of thinking, although the actual term usually used would be 'flow'. It is easy to mistake what I describe here for what is commonly referred to as being in a state of flow - also described as 'being in the zone'.

Flow, as described in literature, is the ultimate state of focused thinking, and it is an important part of ideation, because it is when you learn, experiment, and physically create with the most effectiveness and joy. When it is in possession of flow, your mind has a singular direction, and your progress will become immediately evident. It is like the ranger is surfing, riding a big exciting wave of deliberate advancement! Can you *feel* it?

The ultimate state of the diffused mode of thinking is something very different, and here I would like to take the opportunity to introduce a new expression to define this state: to 'float'. As you float, your mind has no direction at all, and there is no deliberate plan to make progress of any kind.

When you are in a state of float, it is as if the ranger has traded the surfboard for an air mattress. Laying on its stomach looking down, it is now aimlessly floating around above an amazing coral reef, which essentially is the equivalent of an underwater tropical rainforest, indulging its endless and beautiful variety. Can you *see* it?

The meaning of this chapter is for you to understand the importance, and significant benefits, of being able to *feel and see* your own mind and how it operates, from a point-of-view relevant to ideation. Flow and float can both be considered 'peak experiences' (also referred to as states of 'transient hypofrontality' in the scientific literature), but exist on opposite sides of the diffused<->focused spectrum.

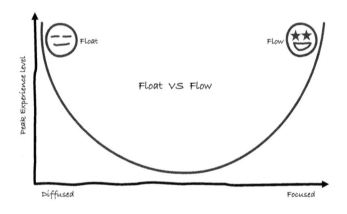

The forest with a ranger analogy is, of course, by no means a complete picture of how your brain and thinking works. But I hope that it can serve as a thought provocation strong enough to question some of your current behaviours, and inspirational enough to get you started on some new ones. Below are two examples to begin this process.

Consider brainstorming workshops at work. What is

the goal of such activities? It is usually to come up with a great idea, a solution to some difficult problem. Now think about what kind of situation you put your ranger in, within that conference room, with your colleagues, and a plan to innovate. It is 100% focused thinking mode, right?

You will focus on the subject matter, on what your colleagues say, on how they perceive you, what you say and do, and so on. Brainstorming sessions and conference rooms are, by design, the worst possible environment for outside-the-box thinking, at least from a neurological perspective. You are, quite literally, trying to think inside a box...

That is not to say that such meetings are useless, but instead that the goal should not be focused on collective ideation. Rather, the agenda should be centred on learning and exploring the problem at hand, and the most non-obvious aspects of it.

Consider what you have just learned about the forest and the ranger. If you use brainstorming sessions to plant as many new and diverse trees as possible, which relate in some shape or form to the problem that you are trying to solve, you increase the probability of the ranger making an unexpected discovery in an hour or two (or days, or weeks...) as it wanders off into diffused mode.

And the same is true for your colleagues, by the way, so the collective probability of making a breakthrough is much larger if you focus on diverse learning and inspiration, rather than group ideation, in such brainstorming workshops.

For the second example, let us consider how most people think about learning new things, so that they can be more innovative. The usual pattern is to be stuck in a monoculture mind (we all are at times, and to varying degrees), and therefore we feel uncreative and 'boxed in'. So we look at other people in the same position as ourselves, our peers essentially, and focus on the ones that appear to be capable of thinking outside the box.

We observe how they present great ideas to use AI, robotics, bioengineering, or whatever the current hype might be. Consequently, we come up with a plan to learn more about these things ourselves, so that we can be as creative and successful as the peers that we respect.

This way of thinking is completely logical, and to some extent it works, as long as there is still a lot to be discovered in the nascent areas we start learning about. But it is a short-sighted and half-baked solution to the ambition of becoming a true outside the box thinker. I have already mentioned Musk and Lamarr as examples of mono/polyculture mix practitioners, but perhaps the ultimate (known) creative thinker in history is Leonardo da Vinci.

The preserved works of Da Vinci can teach us a very important lesson: he did not seem to place any specific value on any particular thing that he set out to learn. He simply wanted to acquire knowledge about everything in the universe, for no particular reason other than to grow an amazing forest in his mind. And, of course, that powered his supreme intellectual output; his creativity.

Da Vinci, Musk, and Lamarr essentially collectively teach us that the value of knowledge increases with the diversity of the context in which it exists.

So, in summary, don't be picky! Just start learning about anything and everything, for no other reason than to cultivate a beautiful and wild mind. Have no interests, but interest itself! And make sure not to get stuck for too long on any particular subject; move on and increase diversity in your neurological rainforest.

If you feel an urge to be efficient in this process, keep reading to find my solution to that conundrum in the next few chapters.

Think like a DJ

The forest analogy is useful for understanding how the brain deals with new information, as well as for illustrating the great benefits of diversity in driving innovation and novel thinking. But it fails to accurately describe how one should think and act to cultivate a rich and accessible mental polyculture; a rainforest of the mind. For this purpose, I have constructed a different analogy: to think like a DJ!

Let me start by defining the term 'DJ', and connect it to some fundamental innovation philosophy.

Firstly, by 'DJ', I mean more the artistic, remix-making and song-writing kind, and less (in fact, not at all!) the popular song A to popular song B mixing kind. But, nonetheless, the mixing of sounds and the collecting of songs are essentials in this analogy, which is why 'DJ' is more appropriate than 'songwriter', or simply 'artist'.

Secondly, this analogy is rooted in what could arguably be called the 'Newtonian innovation philosophy'. Newton wrote the following in a letter to Robert Hooke, way back in 1675: "If I have seen further it is by standing on the shoulders of giants." He is basically saying, "all of my new ideas are based on already existing ideas", which is very much how I think about ideation and innovation.

Perhaps a few rare ideas are completely novel and born from nothing. But the vast majority of new things are firmly rooted in already existing things. Ideating is remixing. This statement finds support in the fact that science has revealed that dreams are entirely constructed from memories. Even the most revolutionary breakthrough ideas are rooted in, or influenced by, the ideas of the paradigm from which they are breaking away. So let us start thinking like DJs!

Great DJs care about two things. We can call them variables - sounds (or songs, records) and mixing skills. Sounds are very much like the trees in the forest analogy; they are pieces of information. But mixing skills is a new concept that does not really fit into the forest story. Mixing skills refers to the ability to combine sounds in a masterful way. These two variables are the DJ's success multipliers, which equally increase the probability of creating something new and awesome.

The more sounds that a DJ has collected, organised and internalised, the more raw material they have to work with. Great DJs are often obsessed with collecting records and creating reference points to the sounds that they discover. The beats per minute, the instruments, the genre, and so on.

Even though this approach may not be how the rest of the world sees it, this is knowledge work. And it is hard work! All DJs have some kind of genre specialisation; ie. one or a few monocultures in their repertoire. But the most creative DJs also collect widely different and strange sounds; ie. they ensure that they also have an inspiring, dynamic polyculture of sounds in their heads, crates and harddrives.

But DJs cannot only collect sounds. They also need to become masters of mixing them - the second multiplier. I call this a multiplier simply because the better that you are at mixing, the more different and interesting things you can do with your raw material. If you have a thousand sounds, and you learn one new mixing technique, then you have a thousand to the power of a thousand new possibilities to use existing sounds (ideas), and create new remixes (innovations). As you can imagine, this soon multiplies into an array of new ideas and directions, which essentially manifests itself as creativity.

Looking at what is required for these two key activities, collecting sounds and learning how to mix them, is very useful for garnering an impression of the work involved in becoming a great creative thinker. Learning new things - corresponding to collecting sounds - is hard work that requires discipline and study, but it is easy to structure and internalise.

Learning ideation on the other hand - equivalent to

mixing in this analogy - is a grinding and abstract marathon about which it is very hard to write a useful manual. Consider the following metaphorical examples:

I have sound "A", and you want it too. Well, go online and search for "A"; voilà - now you can have it too. But how can I teach you, in a similarly effective and efficient way, to creatively 'scratch' a sound and mix it into another? "Put your hand on the player, find the sound, and move your hand back and forth." The result would probably sound awful, and far from the masterful DJ's scratch-mix. Ideation, like DJ-mixing, requires long hours of practice and experimentation, not to mention bucketloads of 'failure'. But, make no mistake, anyone can learn these crafts!

To gain an even deeper understanding of how this long-term collecting and mixing works, let us consider a few very famous words by Steve Jobs: "You can't connect the dots looking forward, you can only connect them looking backward."

This may sound like a dichotomy given the DJ analogy, a DJ's job is, after all, to 'connect', as in mix, the 'dots', as in sounds. But it is, in fact, not at all a contradiction. No DJ ever accurately predicted at the beginning of their career which sounds would come together in the future to bring them fame and fortune. They can only make sense of their collecting and mixing efforts looking back. Understanding this leads to the next big insight for DJs and innovators alike: experimentation is the mother of all great insights and their ensuing ideas!

What is missing in the DJ analogy up to this point is a crucial component of ideation - feedback, the critical answer to the question: "Will it work?". This is another reason why a DJ is a better analogy for being an innovator than, for example, a classic rock band. Because a good DJ is a *super-agile* experimenter. They do not record a full-length album, release it to the world, and then hope for the best. They discover an interesting mix of sounds in their little basement studio in the afternoon, then try it on an audience at the club in the evening. If the feedback is great - ie. if people dance and go crazy - the DJ adds this sound to something already cooking from last week, and soon they have the next big DJ hit song ready for release.

Great ideators engage in this type of frequent experimentation too. But let us not forget that it mostly ends up with failure. Or, rather, with learning what does not work, so not really failure, as previously discussed. But, equally, not a straight road to success. It is, by the way, not always the idea, but the experiment itself, that fails to deliver success. For example, the DJ may be playing for the wrong audience on this particular evening, which is why it is essential to iterate experiments.

Michael Jordan, who needs no introduction, is often said to hold the record for the most successful as well as the most missed shots in the NBA. The latter is not true (close though) but makes for an interesting observation: the frequency of making experiments matters a lot in becoming successful, at anything really. But especially at creative thinking (or ball throwing).

This also reiterates the point, made earlier in the book, that we cannot, or should not, view each of Jordan's shots in isolation. Jordan made 49.7% of the field goals that he attempted in his career. But it is not that he succeeded 12,192 times, and failed 12,345 times, rather these 24,537 shots were all part of the same collective process of mastery (along with training, nutrition, and countless other aspects of Jordan's life), just as Edison learnt from his so-called 'failed' experiments.

Coming back to the DJ analogy, we can relearn an already established key insight from this: efficiency is innovation's greatest enemy! If dots can only be connected in hindsight, how can sounds be collected efficiently? Can you efficiently learn that scratch-mix that I described before? No, no, no! Rather, it pays off to be inefficient, but diverse, in your approach to innovation.

The dangers of efficiency

I think the insight that efficiency and discovery actually are subject to the 'tyranny of the OR' (you cannot have both) explains a lot of the problems with innovation in our society, especially in large organisations. We optimise for efficiency in so many ways, from delivering babies to hospice care, and everything in between. This seems logical, as only a few human activities sound strange when placed in an efficiency context. Efficient love-making. Efficient dying. Efficient dancing. Efficient laughter...

'Efficient innovation' does not sound so strange, though, but it is an absolute oxymoron! I once walked away from a very lucrative consulting deal because the client explicitly insisted that what the organisation needed was an efficient innovation strategy. My response was that I could help them establish an *effective* innovation strategy by optimising their key activities for the exact opposite outcome: novelty. But I was ignored! Since then, a lot of my thinking around this subject has matured, and perhaps with this book as their guide, they would agree.

But why is efficiency such a bad thing for ideation, creativity and innovation? To develop an understanding of this, we can examine the *first principles* of these concepts. To be efficient, which to be clear is not by any means an inherently bad thing, means to optimise the resource-use per output of something. We humans have figured out that the most efficient way to accomplish something, indeed virtually anything, is to standardise and copy that thing.

So the first principles of efficiency are to know the outcome beforehand, and to not deviate from that expected outcome when producing (ie. copying) it. From an individual's perspective, efficiency requires an external answer, a blueprint.

Ideation, creativity and innovation all share at least one core quality - novelty. So what are the first principles of novelty? By definition, we cannot know the new outcome beforehand. Therefore, we must deviate from any established ways of producing anything expected, which means that individuals engaged in these activities must search for internal answers.

Broken down into fundamental building blocks in this way, it becomes clear that efficiency and novelty are in fact complete opposites. The internet made up a great Albert

Einstein quote that fits perfectly here: "Logic will get you from A to B; imagination will get you everywhere." (Trivia: Almost no Albert Einstein quote you have seen online is actually something that the famous scientist said. Many of these "quotes" were in fact invented by Richard Alpert, also known as guru Baba Ram Dass.)

It is very hard to break away from the habit of optimising for efficiency, for good reason. Our lazy brains preserve huge amounts of energy every day by utilising the single-optimal-answer, or 'blueprint heuristic', and simply copying an already known outcome. For example: how do you like your morning coffee? Bam - you have an answer. But how do you know that you like it best black? Or with a few drops of milk? Have you tried it with ketchup? Or a tablespoon of sand? Or snorting it rather than drinking it?

The insight here is that the question can be addressed differently than the way you intuitively answer it; ie. "black" or "with a few drops of milk", due to the always present single-optimal-answer heuristic and your brain's laziness. The alternative answer would be something like: "I do not yet know how I like it best, because I have not tried all possible combinations." But you have adopted an efficient coffee habit, with an outcome that is predictable and easily repeated.

Just by reflecting on this one simple example, I think you can begin to see how this thought pattern repeats over and over again during our days, weeks, years, and entire lives. The more you resist acceptance of the answers provided by this heuristic, the more opportunities for creative thinking will present themselves in your life.

I often come back to one short sentence that has the power to derail efficient but uninspired behaviour and thinking, at least for me: "How do I know what I know?". How do I know that I like coffee with a splash of milk best? The truth is that I don't really know. But with that insight, I can convince my brain to trade efficiency for novelty, and run yet another interesting experiment.

This is also a good place to come back to what I promised you in the introduction of this book – to expand on how Bayes' theorem of conditional probabilities is relevant to refer to as a sort of an *Ideation Equation*. Bayes' theorem, or Bayes' rule as it is often called, mathematically describes how probabilities for an event change with the knowledge of the conditions of previous events. As it turns out, Bayes' rule is directly applicable to the method of ideation you are learning about here, since it relies on 'dots' being 'connected'.

Think of it like this: in a hypothetical future, a phenomenal innovation is going to be the combination of banana peels and used tea bags into fusion reactor fuel. Pretty awesome. Now ask yourself these three questions:

What is the probability for any random person to come up with such an idea? It is a pretty unique idea, so maybe your answer without any additional information is one in eight billion? Effectively, one person of all currently living persons, at the time of writing. It is a guess as good as any, and a good place to start to understand how Bayes' rule works.

Now ask yourself, what is the probability for a person to come up with this idea, if they have read the Wikipedia page about banana peels? That changes the probability a lot from the previous one in eight billion, even if it is hard to say by how much. But think of it like this: you are much more likely to conceive of this idea if you are part of the insightful subpopulation on earth that knows all there is to know about banana peels.

Lastly, what might the probability be of coming up with this fabulous innovation if you have knowledge about both banana peels and the intricacies of used tea bags? Now, intuitively, the probability is even less astronomical!

Hopefully, you are beginning to see a pattern here. The probability of the ranger making an interesting match of trees in your mind's forest is conditioned on the amount and diversity of the trees that you have planted. The probability of the DJ making a mix experiment that creates the next big genre of electronic dance music is based on the amount and the diversity of sounds in their collection. In a systematic approach to get better at 'connecting the dots', the probability of making great connections is conditioned on the dots available. Raw material is not everything, but it is an essential ingredient in *The Ideation Equation*.

There is actually one additional aspect related to Bayes' rule to consider, but I need to introduce a couple more concepts before we can explore that. So, to be continued...

DJs hang out with other DJs

I must return to the DJ analogy again, because there is something that DJs do, which rangers typically do not - at least not the kind of ranger that fits in my forest analogy. That is to hang out with other DJs - and this habit has a big impact on their success!

It is a fact of life that we have a tendency to become more like the people we hang out with. There is even a scientific term for this phenomenon: the social proximity effect. And if we have a mutual admiration of one another, and the features and peculiarities of our particular way of being, we humans also have a tendency to radicalise each other.

This word, to 'radicalise', is nowadays mostly associated with negative influences and outcomes in society, especially around religious extremism and terrorism. But let us not forget that there is radical art and music created by small groups of highly creative people, who inspire each other to go further and further into exciting and insightful new territory. And there is radical innovation and research that often originates in small labs or garages, where a handful of people bring out the best, most radical thinking in each other.

DJs hang out with other DJs not only because it is fun, but also because it makes them better DJs. The same is true for you. If your goal is to become a much more creative thinker, you should make sure that you have some truly creative friends to hang out with. That may not necessarily mean your most creative colleague or friend, or any other person you view as more creative than you. Rather, you should try to find a bunch of people that can *radically* impact your way of thinking. Perhaps that is a colleague, or an existing friend, but in most cases I would assert that it is not, and that you need to search beyond your established social network.

How this works is beautifully described in Rasmus Ankersen's book *The Gold Mine Effect* (Icon Books, 2013). Why are the world's best skiers from a small town in Sweden? The best runners from a village in Kenya? The rates of tech-unicorn founders from Stanford University significantly higher than from other universities?

Even if great ideas often come to us during moments of solitude, the people that we surround ourselves with become part of our 'dot matrix'. Therefore, hanging out with people that are great 'ideators' will have a profound positive impact on you, if indeed you aspire to become an awesome outside the box thinker.

But you should also prepare yourself for change in your already established social life, as you explore *The Ideation Equation* more deeply. To consistently think outside the box means becoming a nonconformist by most social standards, and that may have adverse consequences. For example, in many organisations the most innovative people are portrayed as troublemakers, slackers, or even clowns, and it is not uncommon in my experience for creative thinkers to be 'cancelled'.

So it can be lonely to be creative, not just because of cancel culture, but also because a natural consequence of thinking significantly differently to most people is that few other people will understand you. As your creative universe grows bigger, you may feel that your social circles shrink, which is a big reason why places such as San Francisco, New York, Berlin, Jerusalem, and Shanghai have become hubs for creative people and creativity itself. What may be regarded as 'weird' in your hometown is seen as completely normal and expected in such communities.

In his book *Where good ideas come from - The natural history of innovation* (Riverhead Books, 2010), Steven Johnson makes an excellent point about this aspect of creative hubs, but from a different perspective. He argues that big cities create *social habits* that increase the probability of creative thinking, thus making its native citizens more likely to be creative.

But there is surely more to this phenomenon than population density alone. If there was not, then the most populated areas in the world would be the most innovative, and that is not the case. It is essentially the same counter-argument, as with the myth of resource constraints as an innovation booster, that I raised previously.

Sure enough, Johnson goes on to describe additional conditions that, translated into *The Ideation Equation* lingo, sound a lot like 'urban rainforest' environments. And that makes perfect sense, if you think about it. Every tree we have planted inside our minds is a representation of either an experience of the outside world, or an internal cross-pollination of such trees.

So if we live in an environment full of diverse experiences, and our habit is to receive rather than block out the world around us, then a more diverse internal world is the natural outcome. To actively observe the material world in such environments is a great way to always be learning new things, but the serious DJ's best strategy is to find as many other DJs as possible, and hang out with them.

I have come to the conclusion that there are no substitutes for these environments, and certainly not online social networks, video-meeting tools, and metaverse worlds, as some people may believe. That does not mean that creativity cannot blossom in smaller cities, rural villages, or even in remote single households. But, as explained by Bayes' rule, the conditions in culturally diverse densely populated areas are more favourable for creative thinking to appear, which is largely consistent with, for example, the locations where most disruptive innovations emerge.

A highly personal note is that this aspect of developing creative thinking has always been a barrier for me, simply because I do not enjoy big-city life. In the late 90s, my ambitions for a creative career in the music industry took me to New York. I hated it! There was no way that I could naturally 'zone out' in all the noise and the high tempo of life in the Big Apple.

A few years later, I tried to live in Stockholm, which was more stressful, but hardly more diverse than my hometown Gothenburg, so I moved back. A decade later, the fintech startup I founded, and was then leading as CEO, took me to Silicon Valley, which I liked for a while but ultimately, not enough.

Now I have come to terms with the fact that, for me, the environment to enable my mind to float is more important than being constantly submerged in a high-pace and high-diversity place. I accept the limit that may put on my ability to learn random new things, and the potentially missed serendipitous moments. I am still a mental DJ, and I hang out with a bunch of pretty awesome other intellectual DJs in Gothenburg. And London, Berlin, New York, Nairobi, Shanghai, and other creative hubs are just hours away when I need to fill up on new 'dots'.

How to catch ideas

This chapter of *The Ideation Equation* was, by far, the most difficult one to write. And it may well be the hardest one for you to grasp as well. This is because, from a neuro-scientific perspective, the long-term aspects of ideation and creativity are not yet understood.

If you think about the concepts explored so far - focused thinking, diffused thinking, the act of learning new things, recognising biases and doing something about them - these are all in-the-moment thinking states, or activities that can be studied 'under a microscope', as they unfold. But how something you learned last year, something that inspired you this afternoon, and something you needed to find a solution for over the past month, are creatively stitched together over these time-boundaries - that is still largely a scientific mystery.

It is not easy to intuitively understand what happens when dots connect in our brains either, so as explorers of the neuro-natural ideation method that I refer to as *The Ideation Equation*, we are left with very little to hold on to for this part of the process, in terms of facts as well as intuitions. Even coming up with a good analogy has been very hard, so the best way to shine some light on how to capture ideas is probably to take you through my research and thinking process.

There are essentially two main ingredients involved in the act of catching our brain's ideas: the emergence of an idea, and the consciousness necessary to be aware of it. Emergence is a good place to start, because it is a way to think about ideas where intuition and science overlaps.

The concept of emergence is essential in biology, and represents a mental model that applies to almost every complexity one can conceive, including ideation. A tree is an example of an emergence, springing from the seed, shaped by its DNA, impacted during its development by wind, water, sunlight, and a myriad of other factors. One can never truly foresee the final shape of the tree; it is an emergent structure.

Ideas, too, are such emergent structures. They have DNA, inherited from the inspiring dots connected; the trees in your inner forest that cross-pollinated them. But on their way to our consciousness, during emergence, ideas are also shaped by our beliefs and values, by our moods and feelings, and countless other seemingly unrelated factors. One way to illustrate this is to imagine two people who have had the exact same life experiences, from which they have derived identical knowledge.

But even in this incredible scenario, do we believe that the two parties would come up with exactly the same ideas? Probably, the shared DNA would shine through, like the specificities of a particular species of tree, but still the individually emerging ideas would remain discretely distinguishable and unique creations.

The emergence of creative ideas occurs when a particular neural network in our brains is activated. This cluster of neurons is often referred to as 'the default mode network' for some reason, which clearly is not to be considered pedagogic since most people would not see creative thinking as their default mode of thought. (The logic is actually that 'default' means 'resting state').

You may have guessed that the default mode network is active during diffused thinking, so to ensure that I minimise confusion from this point onwards, I will continue to refer to 'diffused thinking' that has been used throughout this book, and not 'the default mode network'. However, there is an important reason for bringing the default mode network up in this particular chapter, which I will return to in just a few paragraphs.

Besides emergence, consciousness is another important concept that we also need to explore further. Unfortunately, consciousness is even less well understood scientifically than the emergence of ideas. The scientific community has not even been able to agree on where consciousness originates, other than it involves some nebulous combination of the brain and nervous system.

A neat observation is that consciousness is itself an emergence, which is probably why it is so hard to study. When does a tree become a tree? When its first branch grows? When the first leaf blossom? Is the seed already a tree? Or is a tree represented by its DNA, or perhaps the specific genes that distinguish it from other plants? Can we ask similar questions about our consciousness?

But, intuitively, we have some grasp of what constitutes consciousness, or at least the practical implications of being conscious, so we can still explore the concept from this angle, without necessarily being able to truly nail down its origin. If consciousness is similar, perhaps even equal, to being aware of things - oneself, the experience in the current moment, the world at large - then being highly focused is to be in a high state of consciousness. Which, of course, relates to the focused mode of thinking, and flow, to complicate matters!

In the focused mode of thinking, a different neural network takes precedence: the 'executive control network'. As some consolation, this cluster of neurons at least has a more intuitive name than the default mode network! The executive control network is both our friend and foe as ideators. Without it, we essentially cannot pick up ideas that emerge from our default mode network, because it is linked to our sense-making consciousness. But it is also executing heuristics, judgement, and all kinds of other limiting mind tricks. It is basically one of the mechanisms that keeps the box firmly enclosed around our thoughts. In other words, it is essential that we use our executive control network thoughtfully, and with precision.

Let me outline the reason why I think it is necessary to complicate this issue by introducing these two neural networks, rather than sticking to the focused and diffused modes of thinking as concepts. It has been found that those highly creative people who have big ideas that work in real life, and not just in imagination, have a higher interconnectedness between these two neural networks than other people. This is not as simple as saying that they can think in focused and diffused mode simultaneously, because they cannot, as far as anyone knows at least. Rather, they are able to 'keep the lights on' in the executive control network, even if they fully enter the diffused mode of thinking, into a state of float.

Once we have an understanding of these things, the essential question becomes: how can we develop this communication between our different neural networks? So that we can nurture the idea-emergence process as much as possible, while using our consciousness constructively to pick the fruits, as well as provide further nutrients to the process?

Ideally, explaining how I do this myself would be best

executed with another analogy, and I shall provide one imminently. I should mention first that I find this character less colourful than the ranger and the DJ, yet, with an accurate job description. I first had the idea of describing its role as a 'mind ninja'; someone that would sneak around in the forest and spy on the ranger on its random walks. But the assassination part of that analogy became, well, weird. So perhaps a 'secret agent' would work better? Somewhat, yes, but that too would miss the point regarding communication between the two neural networks.

What I finally settled for was - get ready for it - the psychoanalyst! Luckily, the psychoanalyst does not need as much space in this book as the ranger and the DJ, but let us explore what he does in a few paragraphs. (By the way, 'he' is a he simply because he is another 'me' inside my head. Yours may be a she, or a they - psychoanalysts come in all shapes, sizes, and genders.)

This analogy came to mind while I was reading about the work of Arthur Koestler, who once stated that: "creative activity could be described as a type of learning process where teacher and pupil are located in the same individual". Essentially, this is exactly the same concept that appears in psychoanalysis. A common perception is that the psychoanalyst is the teacher, but they are, in fact, just the facilitator of the process. In psychoanalysis, you teach yourself about your inner workings, with the help of a highly-skilled guide asking you carefully crafted questions to lead the way, or at least that is my personal experience.

The psychoanalyst-you, inside your head, is essentially a very gentle observer, and an influencer too when needed. A skilled psychoanalyst will enable your ranger to explore the forest, at a distance, but not so far away as to lose contact. They need to understand where your thoughts are, and in which direction those thoughts are moving. The psychoanalyst oversees the emergence process, and is trained to not interfere, as long as something interesting is brewing.

This is a difficult mental task, because the psychoanalyst is employed in the executive control network department, where the Head of Heuristics and the VP of Cognitive Biases also work. And they, plus hordes of other mental troublemakers, love to storm into the psychoanalyst's office, and disturb, bully, and sabotage its sessions. That is why the psychoanalyst likes to work at night, when the department is empty, and only his tiny office is lit up. With no one else around, they log into the big system: 'conscious-dot-ness', and are able to take notes, and provide gentle guidance without disturbance, both to and from the neighbouring default mode network department.

However, this is where the psychoanalysis analogy falls apart to some degree, because the subject being analysed would, in real life, be reclining on some comfy piece of plush furniture, while introvertly exploring their thoughts, feelings, and experiences. But in the default mode network department there is a major party going on! Actually, one could say that an epic evening is... emerging. New impressions are being thrown around, random connections are being tested, and oftentimes the ranger is engaging in multiple seemingly nonsensical conversations with itself. If the lights are out, mostly, in the executive wing there is, by contrast, a disco-bonanza in the default department!

You may now be thinking something along these lines: "how do I interpret all of this, and incorporate it into some practical advice?". That is a good question, and one that I wish was easier to answer than is my experience. But my general advice would be to focus on controlling your consciousness, and let the emergence process take care of itself.

How many wild parties they throw at the default mode network department is largely a function of your learning activities, along with the development of your habit of allowing the ranger to go for random walks. Your inner psychoanalyst, on the other hand, may not even exist yet! Probably, that is where you should concentrate your focus. Luckily, there is an entire chapter dedicated to that in part three of *The Ideation Equation*!

I will now park the default mode and executive control networks as concepts, and return to discussing focused and diffused modes of thinking, when applicable. The reason for this is that while these thinking modes can be seen as binary concepts, that is, one or the other is active and the opposite passive at any given time; many different neural networks are involved in both these thinking modes.

In other words, there is no clear way to divide the brain physically, through its many networks, between creative thinking and executive functioning. And certainly not by referring to the left and the right hemispheres; that designation of thinking abilities was long since abandoned in the scientific community. Many networks, functions, and regions of the brain are shared between the different modes of thinking, but what really distinguishes them are which networks dominate the internal processes at any given moment. And that seems to be a highly complex dance that we do not completely understand yet.

Taking control

By now, I hope you begin to see what *The Ideation Equation* entails. The vast and diverse collection of dots; the habit to zone out and float - to allow your mind to wander without a plan or any pressure; and the skill to observe and gently influence your diffused thinking process. But, so far, that is about all the control of the process that you have. If you are like most people, what you really want is to acquire useful ideas, not just entertaining but completely random and stupid ones such as my banana-peels-and-used-tea-bags-fusion-fuel example.

To get more control and develop a sense of trust in your ideation ability, you need to understand and practise two additional concepts, that actually can be seen as sequential steps. Those steps do not come *after* those activities that I have described previously, but are, instead, integrated on a different time scale. What I mean is that dot-collecting, zoning out, and observing your own mind at work, are things that you should be doing constantly, and without any specific plan or end in sight. It is these habits that create a vast rainforest in your mind, and the ability to navigate it.

But when you have an ideation objective, you want control. Also, that ideation objective usually comes with a deadline, or at least a timeframe that isn't open-ended. Taking control (or at least trying to do so) is not something you do all the time, and is therefore different from the steps that I have described previously.

If you are like me, you want more control because you want to creatively solve specific problems. You want those ideas to be wild and big, for sure, but also useful and realisable. So how do you achieve this?

Firstly, you need to create a small and highly saturated monoculture over a relatively short period, with the problem that you intend to solve in the middle.

Secondly, you need to systematically, using the focused rather than the diffused mode of thinking, explore all of the key variables of the problem, relative to your own thinking barriers; i.e. your 'box'. Let us now explore these two activities in more depth.

What I mean by creating a highly saturated monoculture, with a specific problem in the middle, is that I want you to become an expert around the problem you are addressing. That may sound counter-intuitive given my previous praise of the rainforest as a great way to achieve more and better creative thinking. But, using the forest analogy, what you want the ranger to do for you, eventually, is to find at least one, and ideally several, trees in the rainforest that can cross-pollinate the trees in your problem monoculture, and completely change the game.

Another way to explain this logically is to once again examine Bayes' Theorem. I previously explained how the probability to come up with a solution, otherwise referred to as connecting a dot (one of many), is conditional on your exposure to that dot.

For example, in the analogy that I used earlier, you are much more likely to come up with banana peels as part of the solution if you know a great deal about banana peels versus very little about them. So here is the new insight: the same is also true for the problem, which in my hypothetical example was to find a fuel for fusion reactors. And that is not just hypothetically, intuitively true, but a mathematical reality.

Bayes' Rule applied to ideation

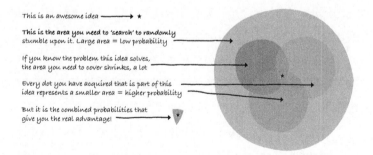

This is an awesome idea ⟶ ★

This is the area you need to 'search' to randomly stumble upon it. Large area = low probability

If you know the problem this idea solves, the area you need to cover shrinks, a lot

Every dot you have acquired that is part of this idea represents a smaller area = higher probability

But it is the combined probabilities that give you the real advantage!

Having vast knowledge about a problem means that you know a lot about its 'connectors' - the peculiarities that the ranger will try to match with other trees in the forest. With many connectors exposed, you have a higher probability to connect useful dots. In the world of conditional probabilities, it is a favourable condition to have expertise about the game that needs changing.

The secret to doing this well is to discipline yourself to not actively seek solutions. What you want to do is to learn everything about the problem; as much and as fast as you possibly can (but not *too* fast). My favourite way of expressing this task is to 'marinate in the problem'. Therefore, you do yourself a service by drilling the problem down to something rather specific. "How can we save the planet?" - that question is too big. "How can we decarbonise the atmosphere?" - that question is still grand, but hopefully small enough to make it feasible for you to become an expert.

A simple way of expressing all of the above is to say that deep insights precede big ideas. But there is a correlation rather than a direct causation between the two. Or perhaps a better way of thinking about the relationship between them is that insights are indirectly causal to ideas. Many people can learn deeply and have the most extraordinary insights about a variety of subjects, but still not be able to come up with any profound ideas that draw on these insights.

If you think of such an individual, they are like a DJ with a rare and super-interesting collection of sounds, but no skills to make an amazing remix. They are not able to connect the dots. They are, mostly, trapped inside a narrow set of thinking barriers - the 'box' that we have mentioned previously. They know everything about their music, even things nobody else has noticed, but they cannot derive anything from that insight.

So in the second step, to break out of your mental box, you can begin to expand the set of connectors that the ranger has access to when on a diffused walk in the forest. When you learn everything there is to learn about the problem at hand, which will occur in focused mode, your brain will apply all sorts of more or less unconscious heuristics, cognitive biases, and filters to try to limit the number of available connectors.

This makes perfect sense from a biological perspective, since it preserves energy and enables the brain to stay focused on its fundamental missions, such as keeping you safe, fed and reproduced. But this process also constructs and reinforces the invisible box in your mind that limits your thinking, and the ranger's options for exploration.

Our mind's toolbox when it comes to limiting our thinking is so diverse and colourful that one could fill multiple volumes with the strategies it employs to stop us from wasting its time and energy. In fact, there are many great books specifically written on cognitive biases that explore those strategies. I will not go into depth on this subject, but I will at least explore a few key themes and what one can do about them.

One category of strategies to limit our thinking that is particularly effective is what I would describe as social status threats. A well-known cognitive bias in this category is the so-called imposter syndrome, which I experience intermittently myself.

You can view the imposter syndrome as your own brain making a threat to your social status, to stop you from doing something that consumes a lot of its energy. It shows up as a little voice in your head saying "who are you to write a book about ideation?", or whatever it is that you are working on. It is implying that you are overconfident, and that you risk falling in the social ranks, so to speak, when people find out about what you are up to.

This self-doubt is, almost invariably, nonsense. And the knowledge that imposter syndrome is just your brain bullshitting you is your most effective weapon against it! The aphorism "whether you believe you can do a thing or not, you are right", often attributed to Henry Ford (but, in fact, centuries old), is well worth contemplating. In terms of ideation, it is literally true, that is, a scientific fact, that a pessimistic or self-diminishing state of mind will cripple your ability to think creatively. That is why you will find an entire chapter on how to deal with fear in part three of this book.

The availability heuristic is a cognitive bias that is a life-saver during our day-to-day activities. It is a way for the brain to save energy by assigning extra relevance to those things that are easiest to recall about something. This typically ensures that the most mundane tasks are done, without wasting resources on deep thinking.

Here is an example that works for most people: I say "caffeine", you think "coffee". But this very useful shortcut gets in the way as we try to uncover as many connectors as possible for a given subject. There are many things we could examine in relation to the word caffeine, including alternative stimulants. But we typically do not, we settle for the answer instantly provided by the lazy lumps of fat contained inside our skulls.

Another very common bias that we all need to deal with is confirmation bias, and this tendency often operates in an unholy alliance with availability heuristics. The biggest problem with confirmation bias is that it works like a reinforcement for the box. Imagine that you begin to learn about some topic where a new approach could unlock a great deal of value. Instantly, due to availability heuristics, you will form thinking boundaries, the box that we have discussed previously, around this topic.

Let us say that the topic is 'fusion fuel', as in my previous example. If you are similar to most people, you now have an image of a fluid in your head, because that state of matter is strongly associated with the word fuel. Rather than asking yourself: "What solids or gases could also be fuel?", you are much more likely to start thinking about "everything that could be fluid fuel", to confirm your initial belief. With every new fluid fuel type that you discover, you will, subconsciously, reinforce that initial belief that fusion fuel must be a fluid, regardless of whether this liquid state is ideally suited to fusion.

If you do not feel that you associate the word fuel with a fluid, you are simply not like most people. I could construct a different example that would work on your brain. For example, I could say that you need to solve a chemical problem using milk, and you would be orders of magnitude more likely to look for solutions to this problem using cow's milk rather than coconut milk, or thinking about the act of milking, or to milk someone's bank account, and so on.

The bottom line is that we are all trapped inside thinking boxes, all the time, this is just not evenly applied since we are all unique beings.

To break the ever-present dance between availability heuristics and confirmation bias in our minds is simple, but not easy. Simple, because all you need to do is to examine your beliefs and then look in the opposite direction. From there, you start to objectively search for the truth. But that is not easy, because we tend to be very attached to our beliefs, we tend to hate being wrong, and we tend to overestimate the rate of exceptions. "But *this time* I am actually right..." which is known as a bias blindspot.

Epic author (I am a big fan) and renowned agnostic Robert Anton Wilson came up with a saying for himself that I try to adhere to as often as possible, as a kind of countermeasure: "I do not believe anything, but I have many suspicions."

What 'to think outside the box' really means is to *expand the box* as much as possible, because we can never really think without relying on beliefs, prior knowledge, availability of information (older memories are generally harder to recall than newer ones), and so on. But inside a greatly expanded box lies exponentially more possibilities than inside the miniscule one that the brain naturally constructs for us in its efforts to save energy.

There is a great way to intuitively understand the concept of the 'expanded box' - just think of the box as an actual box with four sides, like the one in Guilford's experiment. Each side represents a limitation in thinking; for example, the availability heuristic used in my previous example that a fuel is a fluid. As you ask the question, "What solids or gases could also be fuel?", the box changes its form from four sides to six! Because besides fluids you can now include solids and gases in your thinking.

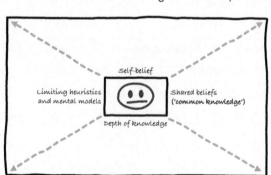

What 'to think outside the box' actually means is to expand the box

However, you are still in a box, it is just much bigger than before. The reality is that we cannot ever truly escape the box around our thinking, but since our minds are virtually limitless we can expand these boxes infinitely!

I will, however, continue to say "think outside the box", since this is the meme we have to accept and live with. It is an axiom now deeply embedded in our culture. If you or I were to say "think in an expanded box", people would probably think that we were trying to be moderately creative, which would miss the point entirely.

To routinely start thinking outside the box, you must develop the habit of asking yourself questions all the time. "Why?" questions are generally great, especially when one's thinking barrier is based around *an impossible problem*. For decades, people exploring space were trapped in a thinking box where one side said that "landing a rocket is impossible". For a long time that was probably true.

But, at some point, it became possible due to new engineering and scientific discoveries. At this point, all anyone had to do to start a revolution in space-flight was to ask "why?". And then follow up with some execution, of course, but that is a different story suitable for another type of book.

All questions are not created equal, though. You should beware of yes/no questions, unless you are prepared to give a box-expanding answer in every situation. Some people advise us to simply say "yes" to everything when we are trying to be creative. But, in my opinion, that is an oversimplification that can cause trouble.

Let me give you a couple of examples: "Can fuel not be a fluid?". Yes. So in this example, a "yes" expands our box. "Am I an impostor?". In this case, you cannot answer "yes" to expand your thinking. The right answer is "no", even if you are an impostor! Because only by continuing on your journey can you become an expert with a unique perspective. Could Elon Musk be regarded as a 'rocket-designer-impostor' the first day, week, month, and year, he spent thinking about using a reusable rocket? Yes. Can he be regarded as such now? Not quite so easily!

Back to the subject of taking control. Usually, the best idea does not arrive promptly as you learn about a problem, and gain insight by expanding your thinking box. These intense learning and sense-making activities are really just preparations. Because the real magic happens when you drop your plan and allow the ranger to roam freely in your mind's rainforest.

But what you have done by intensely studying a subject of interest, and expanding your thinking-box, is to saturate that patch with newly-planted trees close to the ranger's cabin. These trees, that the ranger will pick up on its 'free time', attempting to find good conditions for them within the vast forest for which it is responsible, will all be related to the problem that you wish to solve.

So, in a way, you have tricked your lazy brain to do what

you want by embedding your plan into the new memories that need to be sorted. Furthermore, by exposing as many connectors as possible on each tree, and by viewing those connectors as a variety of roots, you make it much less easy for the ranger to find a spot where the tree can be permanently planted.

What this means is that the ranger will test the compatibility of this tree with other trees in the forest for much longer, and in exponentially more different ways, than if it had merely a few roots, or connectors. What this translates to is, as you have probably guessed, *more ideas!*

The vast majority of those ideas are going to be so nonsensical that they never even reach a consciousness level where you can experience them. My hypothetical fusion fuel example would be such an idea, in that it is so impossible and ridiculous that the ranger instantly sees the bizarreness in it, and moves on. What actually happens in the brain in this case is that too few neurons fire in unison to establish a new significant pattern.

But, eventually, there is going to be what I would like to call a cross-pollination event. Such an event occurs when the ranger tries one of the connectors of a tree, one it has not been able to identify a good place for yet, with something permanently planted in its forest, and the chemistry (literally) is instant and strong! This is Archimedes' "Eureka!" moment in the bathtub. Or the metaphorical (most likely) apple falling on Newton's head. This is how and when the connecting of dots happens, as thousands of neurons fire in sync, in the process establishing a new and strong pattern in the brain.

I have a theory, not scientifically proven to my knowledge but intriguing nonetheless, that we miss the majority of cross-pollination events that could lead to great ideas. This is because most of the time that the ranger spends in diffused mode, we are simply not in a conscious state to receive the idea and internalise it.

This theory could find at least partial support in neuroscience, because we know that the brain performs most of its sorting of new memories during sleep. We also sometimes, at least some of us, wake up with new ideas that formed subconsciously during sleep. Personally, I suspect that those ideas are only a fraction of what useful things the brain cooks up when we're sleeping.

There is also something that I would call idea-déjà vu that could support the above theory, at least conceptually. Sometimes, we get ideas that feel familiar, as if we have had them before, but have only registered a 'shadow' of the idea. Another version of the same phenomenon is when you conceive a great idea, one that feels completely obvious, and you say to yourself: "why have I not thought of that before?!"

Well, perhaps the reason why you feel that it is such an obvious connection to make is because the ranger has already tried it before, perhaps multiple times, but without you being consciously present to pick it up. When you eventually do so, it is a big bang moment for you consciously, but subconsciously you recognise the connection as one already made, and that recognition is what imbues the idea with such familiarity. It is what makes it feel obvious and inevitable.

What you will find as you get better, not just at understanding this neurological process, but also at making use of it and gaining some degree of control, is that the connectors of things you learn about provide the most value. What I mean by that is that, for example, connecting aeroplanes with birds will not really get you very far. It is much more probable that the specific architecture of the bones in birds' wings will find a fruitful connection with your knowledge of micro-cracks in the wings of an aircraft after flying in certain conditions, or something along those lines.

I really like how Frans Johansson frames this in his great book *The Medici Effect* (Harvard Business School Press, 2004). If you have read it, or when you do, you will find that a lot of the concepts resonate with what I am proposing here as *The Ideation Equation*, though this book is more focused on helping you understand your internal wiring.

Halfway through

My good friend David Bailey, who has been one of the invaluable advisors to me as I compiled all of these ideas and insights into a book, made a comment in the margin here: "the perfect book would, at this point, include a pull-out with a map of where I have been, and where I will end up, as well as a self-heating double espresso!"

For all kinds of reasons, both these value-adds are hard to accommodate. But if you, dear valued reader, could be so kind as to serve yourself that double espresso, or equivalent fuel of choice, I will present you with a structured recap of *The Ideation Equation* in the next chapter!

Recap - what is The Ideation Equation?

It is tempting to think of the different activities involved in *The Ideation Equation* as steps, as you probably would if it was an actual mathematical equation, such as Bayes' rule. But thinking in steps would imply neat beginnings and ends, linearity, as well as isolation between these activities, and that is just not an accurate mental model of how this type of ideation works.

Instead of being tidy, ideation is an interconnected, messy, long-term, multi-threaded, non-linear process that is also, as you already know, far from efficient. But it is effective, and it yields unique results that, in aggregate, offset the costs by more than you can imagine. So consider the five things summarised below as key activities involved in

The Ideation Equation, rather than steps in a linear process.

Three of these activities can be considered as long-term *strategies* for building a strong foundation for creative thinking:

Learn about all sorts of random things

Ultimately, this comes down to being curious, and also being willing to invest considerable time in learning about the world. These are the trees in your inner rainforest, the dots you can only connect by looking back. When we analyse breakthrough ideas after the fact, these dots are always far away conceptually from the status quo that we set out to challenge. But we can never tell beforehand in which direction that connection is going to happen.

Make use of your brain's innate ability to connect things

Our brains carry out a lot of tasks, and one of these tasks is to sort the things that we feed them. People generally do not care much about this process, which primarily happens subconsciously, and largely while we sleep. But becoming more aware of the process, and helping our brains engage in this task through diffused thinking while we are awake, will offer access to creativity that you did not know you possessed. This is what connecting the dots really means.

Capture and make sense of your brain's magic

We probably miss most of our brilliant ideas because we are not there to consciously register them. Additionally, the first connection between two dots that eventually turns out to be genius may initially seem like nonsense, and so we discard them as stupid. But to get great ideas, we need to acquire many ideas, and effectively capture them. Therefore, we must train ourselves to gently observe our diffused thinking, and document as many ideas as possible.

The remaining two activities can be classified more accurately as short-term *tactics* to deal with whatever problem you are trying to solve in relation to ideation:

Take control by marinating in a specific challenge

By saturating your brain's processing with information on a specific challenge that you wish to address, you force it to sort through a lot of dots that may hold the key, in the form of a connector, to your next big idea. Ideas are triggered by impressions that your brain, sooner or later, processes. By lining up lots of specific impressions around a narrow topic, you increase the probability of hitting upon an interesting idea around that topic.

Expand your thinking box

Understanding your thinking barriers is key to breaking them up and expanding your thinking into a larger context - a bigger box. This is due to the heuristics and cognitive biases that inevitably impact on our thinking. We cannot ever fully escape these barriers, but we can effectively move them. Shifting them will give you the opportunity to consider more peculiarities about your dots - intriguing details that can serve as future connectors. This will increase the probability of connecting dots in unique and interesting ways.

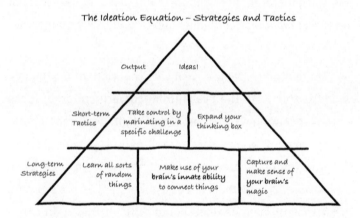

The Ideation Equation – Strategies and Tactics

It may be worth noting here that these five concepts have commonalities with what many academics would call the typical "5-step creative process" - namely, preparation, incubation, illumination, evaluation and verification. But, even more importantly, I want you to reflect on the differences. *The Ideation Equation* goes only so far as the formation of an idea, because that is the essential skill that I am trying to capture and convey with this book.

Evaluation moves us into the domain of critical thinking, and verification into the world of hypothesis-testing; both essential skills for innovators. But I encourage you to think again about the difference between questions with answers that come from *within*, and questions with answers that come from the outside world. You have essentially been trained your whole life for the latter, so give yourself time now to explore your internal abilities.

That is not to say that evaluating, verifying and executing ideas in general are not all important topics. They are just not what *The Ideation Equation* is about, and in my opinion not what creativity is about either.

There is one notable caveat with this distinction, though, which is that both the evaluation and verification of ideas are killer learning activities. Done right, they may create a lot of new dots and connectors, as in the example with Edison's lightbulb. As discussed before, mental models, such as *The Ideation Equation*, or the 5-step creative process, are great tools to help us understand difficult things. But they invariably fall short of accurately and actually describing the full complexity of the real world.

My guess is that you have downed that double espresso by now, and that your energised neurons are making backflips of joy! I also hope that this short but sweet recap of *The Ideation Equation* has provided a clear view of what we have explored so far.

Next, I will take you through four more chapters, designed to augment your knowledge and view of the neuro-natural ideation process, as well as our relationship to ideas as individuals and organisations. This second part of the book then ends with three real-world examples of *The Ideation Equation* at work, before part three takes you through seven

Mind your passion

Follow your passion! How often do we hear this advice, or variants on the theme? Surely, without passion we would not get far at all. But, in reality, our emotional drive and decision-making are far too complex and unpredictable to be followed blindly. In fact, my general advice would be to, instead, not follow your passion, but to 'mind' your passion. I use the word 'mind' rather than 'follow' because to mind something is a two-way street. So what I really want you to do is to pay attention to your passion.

Sometimes, if you are not passionate about an idea then you should not pursue it, because passion is often a necessary source of energy to see things through. But, other times, passion can be a very strong thinking barrier, a cognitive bias making your mental box smaller rather than bigger, even if you feel as if the complete opposite is true.

A long list of such heuristics and cognitive biases are linked to passion in one way or another, such as the optimism effect, the appeal to novelty, the peak-end heuristic, the observer-expectancy effect, the placebo effect, the halo error and the cheerleader effect, the rosy retrospective phenomenon...the list goes on. The reality is that passion is a pretty lousy compass, but also often a necessary fuel for perseverance. To be mindful of your passion is therefore an important practice if you wish to become a master at ideation, for two key reasons:

Firstly, as already mentioned, passion can be a strong contributor to cognitive bias, which makes you think inside a smaller box than is necessary, or, in some cases, a very inaccurate box. But also in a later stage of the process, after new ideas are formed, unchecked passion risks doing more harm than good.

It is my deep experience and firm conviction that one should *never* fall in love with ideas. Because ideas come bundled with decisions, sometimes big ones, and decisions demand a clear direction. Always remember, passion is a lousy compass. Like love, it does not show you what you need to see, but instead shows you what you want to see. Keep your head cool, but your hopes high!

Secondly, if passion for individual ideas should be restricted, the opposite is true for the ideation process. Once you have internalised *The Ideation Equation*, and created the necessary habits to make it stick, then passion makes a huge difference. One can compare this process to learning a new language: falling in love with individual words will only serve the process of making you a less nuanced speaker of the language that you are learning. But falling in love with the language itself will enable you to master all of its peculiarities, and become a poet.

So, to be clear, what I am saying is that to mind your passion for ideation in a broader sense means that you should do what you can to boost it. You can succeed without this passion; you just have to do the work required. But loving that work surely helps, and in some cases it means the difference between becoming good or great at ideation.

This logically leads to the question: can we develop passion for something that we do not instinctively fall in love with immediately? The answer is, of course, yes! The four pieces of advice that I offer below are based on a mix of science and personal experience. I would not say that it is the complete list of things you can do to cultivate passion, though, just to be clear.

Firstly, start practising the thing that you want to fall in love with, such as ideation, on a regular basis. Research has shown that we gradually start to like what we do, or who we spend time with, even if we initially do not have any particularly warm feelings. You may think that "to like is not to be passionate", and that is absolutely correct. But, on the other hand, you cannot love what you do not like. And a passion that is not practised will rapidly fade away, or else transform into bitterness. So the foundation for developing a healthy passion for something is to practise that something.

Secondly, starting to expand your initial interest and general knowledge about the subject can be an extremely constructive process. If it is ideation that you want to become more passionate about (of course, it is!), then dig deeper into the subject after finishing this book. With expertise comes a sense of accomplishment, or pride, and it is natural to love the things of which we are proud.

With expertise also comes a sense of belonging in a social group; what we usually refer to as peers. This group consists of other people with the same expertise that you are developing. Many of the people in this group are going to be naturally passionate about the subject, and by getting to know them some of that passion will inevitably rub off on you too.

Thirdly, prepare yourself for a journey across the infamous chasm. As with anything that is objectively simple, but subjectively not easy, such as relationships, building businesses, or learning new languages, developing passion for ideation or any other complex subject will not be an entirely smooth journey. There will be many fluctuations along the way, but almost invariably you will, at some point, face what many describe as a 'chasm' or an 'abyss': a deep and wide dip in performance, motivation, sense of purpose, and so on. It is very easy to lose whatever passion you have cultivated on your journey when you encounter the chasm, and so it's important to be prepared for this inevitability.

The secret is, of course, to persevere and push through. There is another side to strive for, and by doing the work required you will get there. My advice to prepare for this difficult passage is to adopt passion's slightly less popular cousin - conviction. While passion is exclusively rooted in emotions, conviction can also help you develop a strong foundation in rationality. In fact, I would argue that any healthy conviction should be based on sound rational arguments and empirical facts. And those arguments and facts are much less affected during hardship than your emotions.

So as you run low on passion-fuel on your journey across the chasm, the conviction that you are doing the right thing is a great booster for reaching the other side. In that regard, conviction is stronger than passion, but, honestly, it is also much less fun.

Fourthly, and finally, make the thing that you want to be passionate about a part of your identity. Transition from being an expert in the ideation process to being an 'ideator', or from being an expert speaker in a foreign language to being one with the culture embedded in that language. Let what you do become part of who you are.

But, to be fair, that is only half of the secret of being deeply passionate about what you do. The other half is to love yourself. I did not always love myself, for various reasons. (Perhaps that is the stuff of a future book, who knows). But I decided to make what I was really passionate about part of my identity, and that played a very important role in becoming whole and self-loving.

A big part of this is creating a self-identity with which you can be comfortable, that resonates with you, and that generates personal pride. Once you embody these qualities, your sense of self, and indeed self-love, they naturally blossom, and this then motivates you to invest more energy and passion in your goals. The whole process becomes a virtuous circle.

So besides the many ways that you can grow as a person, mindfully embracing passion and weaving it into your identity can have tremendous positive effects. Just do not let passion alone guide your most consequential decisions in life.

The role of neurochemicals

How many good ideas have you come up with while under stress? How about your colleagues, your friends and family members - how creative are they under stress? As it turns out, the fictional TV persona known as MacGyver, who time and again would invent the most extraordinary things under immense pressure, would be a highly unlikely character in the real world. Because being as predictably creative as he is under stress, again and again, is virtually impossible.

By now, you should intuitively see this, because great creativity flourishes during moments of diffused thinking, which is not necessarily compatible with the state of mind that you tend to enter when stressed. Significant levels of stress tend to invigorate a super-focused mentality, and this doesn't serve the creative process particularly well.

But there is an additional neurological model besides focused and diffused thinking that is worth both exploring and internalising. This model is based on our so-called neurochemical pathways, and is referred to as the 'X framework', or sometimes the 'bowtie framework'. I learned about the X framework at Stanford from professor Baba Shiv, who first came up with this model. In a time when everything intended to challenge the status quo was branded with an X, the X framework sounded like quite a lame name... But it is, in fact, a very clever name, as you will soon see.

The brain has four essential states in terms of hormones, which are related to our state of arousal; not the sexual kind, but our general state of 'alertness', and our feeling of 'pleasantness'. These four states are represented in the X framework, as the four corners of the letter X, and they are inversely connected between left (low-arousal) and right (high-arousal), just like an X.

These two connections are called neurochemical pathways, and they are present in all mammals. Three chemicals regulate how we move around on these pathways: namely, cortisol - the stress hormone, serotonin - the calming hormone, and dopamine - the excitement hormone.

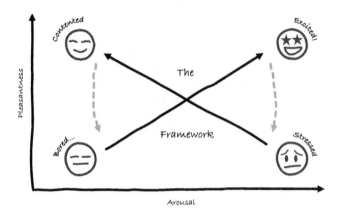

The X framework perfectly explains why *The Ideation Equation* works from a neurochemical perspective. Let us jump into the process involved when you have a problem to solve:

You have spent some time cultivating your internal polyculture, the rainforest in your mind, and learning the art and science of ideation. You can feel your creative abilities growing, but now you want to take control. One day, you decide what problem you should work on, which feels really exciting!

This is where we begin, in a feeling of excitement, which is a high-arousal and pleasant emotional state. Here, you are able to focus and work diligently on learning tons of stuff about the problem. Your brain is swimming in dopamine and you are having a lot of fun! You may even experience the state of mind referred to as 'flow'. This state is in the upper-right corner on the X framework.

But as you study and focus hard on the problem, your dopamine levels begin to drop, and you start to feel that you are not making any further progress. You are supposed to solve this problem, and you are supposed to find a way in, to connect the dots. However, before you know it, you have dropped off the edge of the upper-right tip of the X, and your brain is being drenched in cortisol, also known as the stress hormone, in the lower-right corner.

This happens not because you are bad at staying positive, or anything like that, rather this is the natural direction for your mind to travel on the mammalian neurochemical pathway. In stress mode, you often become even more focused; you may, for example, experience tunnel vision and selective hearing. But your brain is now focused on finding safety from whatever threat it believes is in your immediate vicinity. In this example, your amygdala - the deeply embedded brain region responsible for setting this process in motion - fears a social status threat: that you will fail on your quest to solve the problem, and, consequently, look like an idiot.

There is only one way to move on the X framework - backwards and upwards to the upper-left corner. As you calm down, your cortisol levels drop, and your brain will fill the void with serotonin; a chemical that makes you feel pleasant once more. In this state, you are not particularly focused because your level of arousal is low, but since you are consciously enjoying your newfound state of pleasantness you are still in control.

You reflect on the things that you have learnt on a high

level, you are able to examine your thinking box in a calm and sort of detached way, and your creativity begins to slowly come back online. In this state, you may find your best creativity by 'exploring physically' through activities such as drawing sketches, building models, making prototypes, and other similar pursuits. But, inevitably, you are going to drop off this tip of the X as well, as your brain runs out of serotonin.

Before you know it, you will be bored - the archetypical feeling at the lower-left corner of the X framework. At this point, your levels of cortisol, serotonin and dopamine will all be low. Sounds like a pretty dull place to be, but this is where the magic happens, if you allow it! When the brain discovers its boredom, it craves dopamine, so that it can move up the X again to a high-arousal and pleasant state.

This is the moment when most people turn to some form of distraction, whether this is social media, TV, gaming, eating, or possibly even learning, to get that shot of dopamine. As an expert at ideation, you know better. And it is all related to that cross-pollination event - the eureka moment. Because that event releases a sharp spike of dopamine in your brain!

So by getting bored, and not providing the brain with a dopamine-inducing distraction to move towards the upper-right tip on the X framework, we can incentivise it to come up with cool ideas instead! Because an 'aha-moment' will give the brain the reward that it is craving.

As you start to lose focus, and begin to feel bored, let go of your plans for the ranger. Leave it to roam freely, try to enter a state of float, but stay as close as you can - be your own gentle psychoanalyst. Help your brain stay bored and diffused, yet productive, by stimulating it in particular ways. Take a long shower or a bath, or a walk in a calm and safe environment. If you want to shut the world out, do not listen to an audiobook or regular music, but choose something with a lot of white noise and soft-sounding randomness, such as light rain sounds, slow waves against the shore, winds in the treetops, or something similar.

Eventually, unless you have to interrupt this session of diffused thinking for some reason, your brain will make a clever connection between two or more of the billions of dots it has collected, and that cross-pollination will trigger a rise in dopamine levels and alertness, leading to focused thinking mode and a feeling of pleasantness and enlightenment. Eureka!

Hopefully, one of these dots is going to be related to the problem that you are trying to solve, and the idea is going to be actually useful and brilliant. And you can even say that this is a probability, given the way that the ranger works. But, if it is not, the journey around the X starts again.

It may sound in this example as if going around the X framework is something that I propose we do once, or perhaps twice, for any given problem and corresponding idea. That is, of course, not the case. We run around in this bowtie pattern for all kinds of reasons, multiple times every day, in fact, and most of the time without allowing the brain to fall deeply into diffused thinking mode.

Over the course of an ideation journey for a specific

problem, we may go through this process hundreds, perhaps even thousands of times. Luckily, or unfortunately depending on how you see it, we are all on autopilot around the X. You cannot do much to escape it. But it is absolutely possible to mindfully take advantage of these four stages to maximise the effectiveness of the benefits that each of them offers.

It should be said that the right and the left sides of the X seem to behave rather differently. The right-side drop of dopamine, and attendant rise of cortisol, is often swift and clearly noticeable; while the left-side drop of serotonin, as the brain shifts from calm to bored, is much more gradual and subtle. The diffused mode of thinking does not require boredom; it can be achieved also in a state of pleasantness. But a bored brain seeks a way to move up the X, essentially to 'get high' on dopamine, and the conception of a brilliant idea is one way for it to achieve this goal!

Before I move on to the next subject, I should mention that the number of hormones in our bodies that are regarded as key players that affect our functions and emotions are at least seven, not three (ie. cortisol, dopamine and serotonin).

The X framework is a mental model based on the results of multiple neuroscience studies, that enables us to more easily understand why we feel and act the way we do, and to predict where we may be headed next. But the reality is, of course, orders of magnitude more complex; more interactive, interconnected, and intricate in all conceivable and inconceivable ways.

Regardless of this complexity, I have found the X

framework to be a very valuable tool when trying to understand how our minds work. I suspect that is because these three hormones and neuro-chemical pathways really do take centre stage.

If you can imagine the human mind as a climate system rather than a thinking device, dopamine would be like the sun, cortisol like the wind, and serotonin like the moon. Our thoughts would be like water, and these three forces would constantly move that water around, vaporising it, sweeping it away, condensing it, and pulling it in and out from shore. Many other things affect water, but these three are by far the strongest forces, more or less overshadowing everything else.

The idea spectrum

The process of becoming good at ideation is a very abstract concept for most of us, at least compared to many other things that we aspire to do well. How do you measure ideation? What is good and what is bad when attempting to develop the skill of ideation? What is a favourable frequency for acquiring ideas? Achieving excellence at running, cooking, or selling seem like much more straightforward ambitions; and this initial impression is probably correct.

I have given this notion a great deal of thought: "how do I know that I am good at ideation?" Over the years, I have developed a few fundamental principles and insights that help me to both assess my progress, and guide my strategies to improve. By sharing these thoughts, I hope to bring at least some clarity to the process of addressing these challenging questions.

A first insight, backed by both my personal experience and a lot of empirical evidence, is that one is not evenly good or bad at ideation, as with any other mental or physical activity. Throughout life, even the most creative people experience short bursts of creativity and long stretches of idea-drought. It is therefore important to know and remember that this is normal, and probably even necessary for all other aspects of life to work as intended. Before I understood this, I felt very stressed during less creative periods of my life, a stress that in turn inhibited my creative thinking further. Your ideation ability cannot be forced; it instead needs to be nurtured.

A second insight, or perhaps more of a principle, is that ideas have intrinsic value, purely as ideas. This principle stands in stark contrast to the 'correct' view of the startup and innovation community, where most people with a strong opinion about how innovation and entrepreneurship actually works (ie. everyone in this space) will say things like: "Ideas are nothing, execution is everything." Or, as one of my acquaintances put it: "without execution, even the best ideas are worthless".

To the creative thinker, this should be viewed as nonsense. A great idea is a great idea, regardless of whether it is implemented or not, and history is replete with such examples. Perhaps the best one is Leonardo da Vinci. The Mona Lisa is execution; Da Vinci's notebooks, however, are just ideas. Today, though, we regard those notebooks to be as priceless as the iconic painting.

You may, however, be judged as a fool or a genius, depending on your own implementation of an idea. Perhaps the most famous illustration of this principle is Ignaz Semmelweis' idea that doctors' filthy hands cause infection, for which he was ridiculed. Louis Pasteur had the same idea only a few years later, but was able to implement it in a different way since he had additional compelling evidence.

Pasteur's successful execution does not mean that Semmelweis' idea was less valuable. This is something that the ideator should always keep in mind. Society will label you a fool based on your ideas, and a genius based on your execution, at least during your lifetime. My advice, though, is not to focus on executing well as a creative thinker, so that you receive recognition to feed your ego, but to, instead, ignore external judgement entirely.

If you are not convinced by this principle, consider this analogy: ideas are like streams of water, and the ocean is everything we already know. All streams eventually reach the ocean, at least in this analogy, and once they connect with this enormous body of water, their potential energy is zero. But at a higher altitude, the water could be held up in a dam. There, the water would have potential energy, which could be converted to electricity; i.e. value, if it was released through a turbine. The higher the altitude, the greater the potential energy/value.

As an ideator, your job is to create streams of water at high altitudes with big potential energy. Execution, on the other hand, is about building dams to harness that water, while turbines convert its energy into value, thus representing the business model. This means that even if you do not execute, ideas still have that potential energy.

Some people love to glorify operators and treat ideas like cheap commodities, especially early-stage investors. What those people have not realised, apparently, is that just as the world is full of streams without dams (potential value, but no execution), it is also full of dams where there is no stream in sight (execution, but no potential value). Unfortunately, or perhaps luckily, depending on your perspective, reality is not a meme. And memes do not become reality, no matter how much they resonate with people. Take note, all you meme-loving VCs!

Another important thought provocation along these lines came to me during a lesson at Stanford with Bill Barnett, Professor of Business Leadership, Strategy, and Organizations at Stanford Graduate School of Business. He drew a very simple, but eye-opening, two-by-two matrix in which he classified ideas as right or wrong, and consensus or non-consensus. He went on to say that the measure of right or wrong is empirical; we can only truly know if a new idea works by trying it out in the real world.

People tend to have an opinion, though, long before any empirical evidence arrives. So there is usually a consensus or non-consensus about a particular idea's worth in society and organisations, long before anyone can confirm or deny this with actual data.

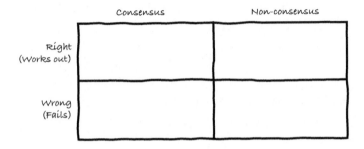

Bill Barnett's Idea Consensus Matrix

Barnett's core point in relation to this is that decisions about which ideas to try out, for example in a company, are mostly based on the consensus opinion. He says that, naturally, organisations do not pursue ideas that the majority of decision-makers in that organisation think are bad, so those ideas are rarely tested in the wild.

Secondly, ideas that those same people think are good ideas are those that do attract resources and endorsement. However, some of the best ideas throughout history, such as Semmelweis' idea about hygiene, were, after the fact, non-consensus ideas. For example, the consensus in the medical community at the time was that the idea was ridiculous, when, with the benefit of hindsight, it was a game-changer.

Here is the important lesson: when ideas are tested for validity in the consensus space (which will only be ideas that we believe to be good) people, as a group, are either all wrong, or all right. Usually, we collectively blame some random external factor if we are wrong as a group, and credit our own genius if we turn out to be right. This is basically the same cause and effect perception that can be observed in sports supporters; it is either "they lost" ('they' meaning your own team) or "we won".

However, people that pursue implementation of non-consensus ideas in which they believe, face completely different consequences. If the idea turns out to be bad, as the opposing collective initially believed, the brave soul that pursued it is labelled a fool. If it instead turns out to be the best idea ever, the individual is regarded as a genius, and a lot of people will claim that they actually supported the idea and the person all along.

I think this is a great mental model for how the world works when it comes to ideas within tribes, such as companies, and how unfit our human psychology is to deal with it as individuals.

Firstly, academics suggest that humans hate to lose about twice as much as we love to win.

Secondly, our tribal status is fundamental for our safety and wellbeing; a threat to our social safety is as real to our amygdala as a tiger or a snake.

Consequently, very few people are either brave, naïve, or crazy enough to pursue, or even talk about, non-consensus ideas. Are you one of them? If not, you should try it. It is not as bad as it sounds.

Based on Professor Barnett's idea consensus/outcome matrix and Tim Urban's *Marketplace of ideas demand curve* (waitbutwhy.com, 2019), I developed what I call the 'idea spectrum' to build a richer mental model for how ideas are treated and mistreated in organisations. This is important for you as an ideator because having a framework to observe your organisation's interactions with (your) ideas gives you two advantages:

Firstly, it provides a tool to rationally distance yourself from your ideas and from the collective.

Secondly, you can use the spectrum as a framework to develop your organisation's ability to deal with ideas in an increasingly sophisticated way.

The idea spectrum is a bell curve shaped visualisation of how ideas are treated in organisations. At the peak of the curve, where most ideas exist, there is a divider, which separates bad ideas to the left, and good ideas to the right. To the far-left we find the occasional super-bad ideas, and to the far-right we find the equally rare super-awesome ideas. But rather than drawing a horizontal line to map out consensus, I asked myself: "what is it that forms people's opinions about the quality of ideas?".

My hypothesis is that people in general will not endorse anything that they do not understand, especially not ideas that also go against their established beliefs, such as with Ignaz Semmelweis. Therefore, people's ability to objectively (even against their own beliefs) assess the viability of ideas is what establishes the consensus.

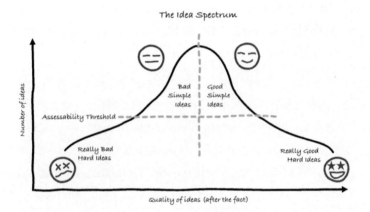

To make a clear point here, consider only these two scenarios:

Firstly, an idea that is easy for the collective to assess as bad because they understand it well, will be labelled as bad. For the sake of the argument, we should consider this a true negative; ie., we trust the organisation's ability to actually predict the outcome as bad with reasonable accuracy.

Secondly, an idea that is hard for the collective to assess as either good or bad, will also likely be labelled as bad. This is, however, a potential false negative – an idea that, if implemented, could lead to extraordinary results!

From this mental model of the relationship between ideas and the collective, it is possible to make a few reasonable hypotheses that are well worth thinking about and working with.

The first hypothesis is that, the ideas in organisations that get the most votes are generally those that are best and most easily understood, which likely makes them close to the peak of the bell curve.

This may seem like a great place to be, but it is most likely not particularly inspiring in reality. Ideas that are easy to assess generally do not change the fundamental rules of the game. They are what is often referred to as 'incremental innovations'. Do not get me wrong, such ideas are not bad. But they will be generated and implemented regardless of any effort to boost them; at least, in any reasonably healthy organisation.

The second hypothesis is that working actively with the ability of decision-makers to assess ideas is a great way to potentially convert some false negatives to true positives. This can then see ideas that an untrained management would have labelled bad, and consequently never implement, instead put to the test by an enlightened management, ultimately turning out to be great. In the visualisation, this exercise means that the ceiling for which ideas the collective is capable of assessing is lowered, so that more extreme ideas can be considered.

A third hypothesis is that the most unconventional and potentially amazing ideas cannot be readily assessed, regardless of how much we train ourselves, or our peers, in forward-thinking. The only way to find out is to try.

The most innovative organisations have adopted strategies to allow ideas in this space to be tested, without any negative consequences for the ideator if any of them turn out to be bad. In fact, some organisations have opted to only pursue ideas that are so original that no one can reliably assess their viability. Because this is the area where unicorns are born, and some people are only interested in unicorns.

With these perspectives on idea-assessability, and their attractiveness for different audiences, let us return to the analogy of thinking of them as streams of water. Imagine a stream flowing from just a few metres above sea-level. Everyone can see how it roars into the ocean. Everyone can easily envision how a dam just a few metres high, and a turbine, could transform the water's potential energy into value.

Now visualise a stream of equal size, but a thousand metres up in a mountain. It is not easy to see, so naturally a lot of people will not believe it is there. That is just the way people are. And, even if they do, it is equally hard to imagine how that dam and turbine should be built and operated. In absence of analytical 'proof', imagination is crucial for breakthrough innovation to take root. Not only for the sender (innovator), but also for the receiver (management).

Big corporations generally go after ten streams right by the ocean, and manage to build and operate seven or eight of them, at best. Venture capital investors, on the other hand, typically try to build ten dams at a thousand metres above sea-level, but only succeed with one or two, or sometimes zero. Specialisation can be a good thing, but economic theory, and a lot of compelling evidence, would suggest that diversifying your bets will render the best average return.

So make many streams of water, both high and low, but not too low. And make sure there is real water in your streams, real value for real people, before you start building your dams and turbines. Remember, it is easier to build a dam where there is a stream, than it is to direct a stream to where there is a dry and dusty dam.

Ideation in real-time

If you are like Daniel, you may find that an objection is eating away at you at this point. He pointed out to me that the way I describe *The Ideation Equation* makes it appear as if I only encounter ideas in solitude, and while in a state of diffused thinking. This surprised him, because his experience is that I can 'think outside the box' in real-time, in workshops with many other people, and even under stress. This is, of course, a very relevant observation, and something that may sound contradictory to much that I have written up to this point. But it is, in fact, a natural effect of implementing *The Ideation Equation*'s core concepts into your life.

But before I can explain this further, I need to make an objection to the objection...or perhaps more of a clarification. Daniel is, of course, right in his observation that I have an above-average ability to come up with ideas in highly focused and dynamic situations. But we need to distinguish between these real-time ideas, and the truly creative ones that arrive via the ranger's random walks in the mind-forest during diffused thinking.

If I were to attempt to rate all of my ideas, compiling a top ten in terms of creativity, potential disruption, value creation, and so on, they would *all* come from moments of zoned-out solitude, and subconscious dot-connecting. That is, during sessions of float.

But that is not to say that all of those other ideas, the ones conceived in real-time to which Daniel refers, are without value. On the contrary, the ability to think outside the box in a social context, with new information being processed and 'connected' in real-time, is extremely valuable, and, perhaps just as importantly, extremely fun!

Thinking about this observation, and the correlation between the ability to have big ideas through diffused thinking, and quick ideas while in a state of focused thinking, I realised that a few key concepts are causal to both of these traits. As I explore these concepts below, you will probably see how a shared causation makes perfect sense.

Firstly, let us consider how the brain processes new information as it arrives. As always, the amygdala has the first say in determining whether or not this new information is a threat to us. As previously discussed, being susceptible to things that could be perceived as threats to our social status constitutes the foundation of a substantial thinking barrier.

This could assume the form of worrying about understanding new information correctly, fearing that what we say (or even think) may sound stupid, or being overly concerned with how our reaction to this new information may offend, or in other ways be negatively perceived by, other people.

These are all natural tendencies in many of us, but to master *The Ideation Equation*, one must overcome such fears and concerns. And once you are freed from them, your ability to process new information in real-time in a focused social context will be greatly enhanced.

Secondly, the next natural concept to consider is your ability to expand your thinking box, not merely by eliminating 'amygdalian disruptions' (fear, anxiety, and the like), but in all possible directions. As a creative thinker, trained in *The Ideation Equation* way of processing 'dots', you have developed a set of simple tools to spot limiting heuristics and thinking barriers. In order to illustrate this, we can use my previous example with fuels.

In a group of people brainstorming around some issue where 'fuel' comes up as a consideration, making the point out loud that all forms of fuel should be considered, across the three forms of matter - liquids, solids and gases - may be perceived as outside the box thinking. As previously discussed, this is an example in which most people will automatically make the assumption that fuel equates to liquid, as this is the form in which we most readily encounter it. This is a classic example of a limiting heuristic, or thinking barrier.

Overcoming this mode of limited intellectual ability in the moment can be achieved via 'reframing', 'inversion' and 'first principles reasoning', which are all real-time thinking tools that can help you to navigate over, around, or through barriers to creative thinking. And there are, of course, many more that you can explore.

Thirdly, as a highly effective (yet in a way inefficient) dot-collector, you always have a wealth of random information at your disposal, and this also applies in a social and focused thinking context, such as workshops or brain-storming sessions. But not only that, you have also developed the habit and intellectual ability of giving your dots many more connectors than would usually be the case with most people.

So not only do you have much more diverse knowledge in your head than the average person, you also have many more possibilities to logically connect them to the issue being discussed in the group. This dot-connecting also works, to some extent, in real-time. However, at least in my experience, it is not likely to render as many creative connections as it may in a diffused mode of thinking.

Fourthly, on your journey to mastering *The Ideation Equation* you have conceived of thousands of ideas, most of them not very useful. But, nonetheless, many of these ideas will become trees in your mind's rainforest, dots waiting for the right moment to make useful connections.

When Daniel or other people perceive me as capable of coming up with amazing creative ideas in real-time, and even under pressure, often what has occurred is that I have connected some half-baked, old idea to the new context and topic presently being discussed, and that it just happens to be way better in this configuration relative to when it was first conceived. This is known as 'idea recycling', and I will take you through it in part three of *The Ideation Equation*.

Lastly, I previously described creative thinking as being like a muscle, or rather a complete arm with many muscles, with this muscular collection making the arm strong and agile. This full-spectrum view of creative thinking also applies to situations where the prerequisites for hitting upon breakthrough ideas are not optimal from a neurological perspective, as in focused social settings, such as workshops and brainstorming sessions.

Let me once again make an analogy with athletic abilities, to illustrate why this more general view on creative capacity applies also to suboptimal conditions. Imagine that you are a professional dancer. Your optimal performance will be enabled by an oakwood floor with just the right response, an ambience temperature of 21 degrees Celsius, and lights and music in perfect sync.

Now to illustrate the conditions that your creative brain must endure in a focused social context, imagine that you are in a snowstorm, on a newly ploughed field, without any music or special lighting. Even if your dance performance is a mere shadow of what you could achieve under optimal conditions, people around you will still perceive your moves and expressions as amazing!

This is exactly how I feel when I am expected to think outside the box 'on command' in innovation workshops, and other similar events. But do not misunderstand me, just as the dancer enjoys twirling through every situation in life, even in the snowstorm and while caked in mud, I also enjoy creative thinking in situations that are far from optimal from a neurological perspective.

It is just important to understand and remember that such sessions are scenarios in which it is unlikely that your *best* performance will emerge from beneath the surface. And, sure enough, almost without exception I will acquire new and better ideas, hours, days or even weeks, after such workshops. Similarly, you may also have, at some point, experienced a 'delayed solution', making you reflect in the aftermath that you "should have said this" or "could have proposed that", rather than what you actually said or did at the time.

Observation and insight may serve as a good conclusion for why the ability to think outside the box in real-time has its own enormous value. These two qualities represent a good way to expose issues and opportunities from a diverse set of viewpoints, rather than seeing everything from merely your own perspective, and, in the process, create new dots for future cross-pollination. The ideas that come up in the workshop itself may not be your best ideas, but they may inspire you, or others, to connect just the right dots further down the line.

The Ideation Equation at work

Now that the five core concepts of *The Ideation Equation*, as well as a handful of related areas of interest, have been uncovered and explored in depth, I want to present you with three accounts of well-documented ideation events where this neuro-natural process was clearly at work.

We have to be aware of what is usually called 'survival bias', though, as we dig into the anecdotes. That is, if we judge *The Ideation Equation* based only on the available stories that seem to portray it in fruitful action, we fail to account for all of the miserable results that it has also rendered, which, precisely because of their misery, never became stories that were cited and repeated.

This kind of bias is, of course, also true for all other ideation frameworks that exist, because the nature of exploring the previously unknown is a risky business. This same bias also applies to almost every insight that we derive from anecdotal learning. I make this comment not to discount the learning value of the stories that follow, but simply to help you see a bigger picture.

How Dmitri Mendeleev came up with the Periodic Table

The Periodic Table may not appear to be the archetypical creative idea in today's society, but at the time of its conception it was a leapfrog achievement in the world of natural science. This was true to a large degree due to the fact that many of the elements that today fill up the table were yet to be discovered. But, with the periodic table as a tool, Mendeleev was able to predict their existence! The story about how this idea came about reveals how all five factors of *The Ideation Equation* played their part.

Mendeleev was a young Russian chemistry professor at the Technical Institute in St. Petersburg, in the mid-to-late 19th century. He had studied in Europe, experiencing the advances in science there, and passionately tried to bring as much of this new knowledge back to his homeland.

But he found teaching contemporary advancements in chemistry difficult, largely because the elements were not classified in a system that described the relationships between them. So Mendeleev began to learn everything he could about the properties of all the known elements; a perfect example of taking control by *marinating in a specific challenge.*

Next, he took advantage of seemingly unrelated, *random knowledge* that he had acquired earlier in his life - the organisation of playing cards in a game of solitaire, also known as patience. By writing down the properties of each element on a card, he was able to try different combinations and principles, easily rearranging them in search of a holistic system.

At the time, it was common knowledge that the elements were to be grouped together based on their basic properties, such as if they were gases or solids, or depending on their atomic mass. But Mendeleev challenged this notion, essentially *expanding his own thinking box,* believing that both properties and atomic mass could be combined within a single system.

One day, when he felt as if his obsessive learning about the elements, and his attempts to organise them into a holistic system, was near a breakthrough, he laid out his cards and began to organise them. Mendeleev continued to try various combinations for three days and nights (we can assume he was in a state of flow), without ever reaching a satisfying result, and finally fell asleep from exhaustion.

In his deep sleep, he later recalled, "I saw in a dream, a table, where all the elements fell into place as required"; an example of *making use of our brain's innate ability to connect things.* It is also worth noting how a state of float seems to have followed a state of flow, leading to the breakthrough idea.

Finally, as Mendeleev woke up from this dream, he immediately drew this table on a piece of paper, which constitutes a perfect example of the fifth activity of *The Ideation Equation*: to capture and *make sense of our brain's magic.* The periodic table is, in common with many profound advances in society, both a highly creative idea and a scientific discovery. It also builds on a foundation of knowledge previously carved out by others, shoulders that Medeleev was able to stand on to achieve what he did.

It can be argued that Mendeleev was an expert in chemistry, and that this expertise alone led him to the discovery of the idea of a periodic table. But the idea is, in fact, a cross-pollination between chemistry and a solitaire tableau. And his challenge of common beliefs within his own guild is also not typical for domain experts. Rather, Mendeleev seems to have been well-attuned to the neuro-natural ideation forces that led him to the right path.

How Kary Mullis came up with PCR

The Polymerase Chain Reaction, PCR, is today an essential part of virtually every procedure related to genetic testing and research. It is a method that allows for the precise and rapid reproduction of DNA molecules.

Many people became familiar with the acronym PCR during the Covid pandemic, since PCR testing was an essential part of diagnosing infections and tracking the spread of the virus. Through a PCR process, the DNA of the virus would be amplified, if present in a sample, and could thus be studied.

Kary Mullis, who invented PCR in 1983, and received the Nobel Prize in Chemistry for his achievement ten years later, has provided a remarkable account of how the idea was conceived. To the non-chemist, this chronicle is quite hard to digest as it contains many references to the use of such things as 'synthetic oligonucleotide', 'dideoxynucleoside triphosphates', and 'bacterial alkaline phosphatase'. But in between these technical terms there is a wonderful story of *The Ideation Equation* at work!

Mullis was an expert in biochemistry, he had a very large and useful monoculture forest, based on that subject, in his mind. But he had also worked as a fiction writer earlier in his life, and managed a bakery during his postdoctoral work. His autobiography also reveals that *he explored a multitude of widely different topics,* and enjoyed designing thought-experiments that challenged common knowledge and broadly held beliefs. Clearly, Mullis was a prolific dot-collector.

The idea for PCR was conceived through one such thought-experiment, as he was driving up a mountain in California, one late spring-evening of 1983. Mullis had *focused on two specific problems* related to genetic analysis, namely the production of DNA sample material (synthetic oligonucleotide) and the need for precise and rapid testing of foetus

DNA, in the search for unfortunate mutations.

As he drove up the mountain, his focused rumination around the specifics of those two problems slipped away, as he recalls: "Unconsciously combining the two problems ... My hands felt the road and the turns. My mind drifted back into the laboratory. DNA chains coiled and floated. Lurid blue and pink images of electric molecules injected themselves somewhere between the mountain road and my eyes."

Mullis continues his account of the event with a profoundly interesting testimony: "I see the lights on the trees, but most of me is watching something else unfolding." Clearly, he is allowing his mind to continue to float, but he is actively observing what is happening. Being a prolific thought-experimenter, his mind is on autopilot, magically *connecting the dots* in his mind that will lead to a new scientific paradigm.

Finally, as every bit of his invention had fallen in place, contained in his thought experiment, Mullis stopped his car by the roadside and contemplated everything it entailed. He ends his story: "I didn't sleep that night...by mid afternoon had settled into a fitful sleep. There were diagrams of PCR reactions on every surface that would take pencil or crayon in my cabin. I woke up in a new world."

(www.karymullis.com)

How Joanne (J. K.) Rowling came up with Harry Potter

The story about how Harry Potter, Hermione Granger, and Ron Weasley came about, is often told as "a sudden, magical flash of inspiration". However, with knowledge of *The Ideation Equation* at our disposal we know better, and can try to reverse-engineer the process, from Rowling's collecting of dots to the capture of the idea.

If we begin with the act of *catching ideas and making sense of them,* Rowling was already at this time a prolific note-taker and idea-organiser. This skill was, in fact, an important part of her key expertise, her intellectual monoculture, which had emerged around writing. From a young age, she had aspirations of becoming an author.

As it were, Rowling did not have pen and paper with her at the time when Harry Potter and his friends arrived inside her mind, but the moment she came home, several hours later, she began documenting her idea for the seven-book series.

The idea for Harry Potter and his adventures came about as Rowling was stuck on a delayed train from Manchester to London. We can speculate that it was perhaps first stressful, then rather comfortable to be on a train and not stuck in a car, and after that, presumably, boring. She recalled that her mind started to wander.

Then: "the idea came out of nowhere and I could see Harry very clearly; this scrawny little boy, and it was the most physical rush of excitement. I've never felt that excited about anything to do with writing. I've never had an idea that gave me such a physical response. So I'm rummaging through this bag to try and find a pen or a pencil or anything. I didn't even have an eyeliner on me. So I just had to sit and think. And for four hours, because the train was delayed, I had all these ideas bubbling up through my head." (BBC, 2002)

So Rowling says "out of nowhere", but we know better - it was the ranger trying to find a good spot for some unsorted experience, a memory, that triggered this idea. We cannot know where "Harry" came from, of course, but we can confidently say that it was from somewhere rather than nowhere.

Note also Rowling's recollection of a physical response, the brain awarding itself with a big shot of dopamine for making such a wonderful connection! Lastly, note her decision to sit and *further explore the idea,* rather than completely losing her float, which she would have if she went to look for pen and paper elsewhere in the train. Instead, she acted like a real *Ideation Equation* master practitioner!

It of course gets tricky to speculate about how, when and where Rowling built up her inner rainforest, which clearly played a large part in the ideation process for Harry Potter. But we know that she took a lot of inspiration from her own life experiences. She grew up in an old stone-house of Victorian Gothic style; at age 10 she joined the local scouts which were organised in groups called 'Fairies', 'Pixies', 'Sprites', 'Elves',

'Gnomes' and 'Imps'; and a year or so later she wrote her first short story *The Seven Cursed Diamonds*.

It is also hard to say how Rowling worked to expand her thinking-box. One could instead argue that the box within which she decided to work is not very expanded, but on the other hand *consistently explored and documented*. The Harry Potter world borrows almost all of its bigger components from previous literature, but, for the most part, with finesse. This creates a familiarity for readers, a box 'to hold on to', which Rowling silver-lined rather than tried to break. And the commercial success of this speaks for itself. It is not always better to be radical.

PART THREE
APPLY

Introduction to part three

Now that you have a better understanding of *The Ideation Equation*, it is time to circle back to the analogy provided in the first part of this book - that creative thinking is like muscles on one of your arms. This third and final part of the book is focused on prescribing methods to help you exercise your creativity-arm, and put *The Ideation Equation* into practice, as well as describing reasons and mitigations for limiting behaviours and thoughts.

Can a handful of habits *really* make you a creative genius? Yes, they can! These habits can help to ensure that you never lose your focus on creativity, and become an outside of the box thinker, capable of generating a steady stream of exciting new ideas. There is a big body of research that suggests that there are many different habits that can increase our creativity.

However, many of these activities are good for us *generally*, not specifically for creative thinking, so I will not dig deeper into habits of this nature. Such studies could claim that sleeping adequately has a positive impact on creativity. This is true, just as sleeping well is favourable for almost anything that we strive to achieve. In this category of good habits, for creativity and other self-improvement, we also find exercising, eating healthily, and meditating; as would be expected, since these things are good for more or less everything.

Rather than examining these more generalised approaches, you will instead find advice on how to cultivate more specific habits, and deal with distinct issues related to ideation, in the following chapters. I should say that much of this advice is based on my own experiences and methods, but it is also verified by the same science that inspired me to write the analogies that we have already explored.

It should also be stated that even though *The Ideation Equation* works the same, more or less, in all humans, since it is based on our neurological circuitry, how we respond to experiences designed to inspire and evolve our thinking can differ widely. In other words, you should take a very individual, personal approach to adopting habits that boost your creativity.

You will also find some repetition of concepts in the following chapters. I have decided to let that be, so that this final part of the book can serve as a standalone blueprint for how to design habits and thinking patterns that increase creativity. So if and when you feel a need to review things, to further accelerate your ideation-ability, my advice is to start with this last part of the book, and look for activities that you could prioritise.

Let go of fear and negativity

Fear really is a double-edged sword. Without fear, we humans would not exist. But equally true is that, without fear, a lot of things would exist that do not exist now. This dichotomy prevails because fear is a highly inaccurate instrument that influences virtually all of our decisions. We all know what we have to choose from when fear comes knocking: fight, flight, or freeze. And when it comes to embracing our creativity, a flight or freeze response is all too common.

I try to teach my kids a fundamental lesson about fear that we all intuitively know, but easily forget, especially in the moment: *fear* and *danger* are not the same thing. Our brains want us to believe that they achieve the same thing, because believing the notion that fear equals danger has helped keep us alive for millions of years. But while there is some overlap between the two, they are not necessarily analogous.

The chronological order of the concepts of fear and danger is, of course, the other way around. Our brains predict potential danger, and release hormones, most notably adrenaline and cortisol, that trigger our fear response. But signalling: "I predict potential danger, please investigate" is far too inefficient for the lazy brain, so it sends a shorter message: "Danger!". Even if we can train our amygdala to be less reactive to some extent, we cannot completely shut down this primal neurological function.

Consequently, we are left with only one option: to deal with our fear. You do not need to consider such things as presenting new and crazy ideas to an audience (often referred to as the *only* thing people in general fear more than dying) to find yourself in an anxious state. Many people feel anxiety and self-doubt in so many situations linked to creativity; for example, trying to induce diffused thinking by walking alone in a forest.

Apart from being attacked by infuriated ants or losing the signal on your phone, what is the danger? When we feel anxious or have self-doubts, which are both manifestations of fear, we should always begin to deal with this by asking the simple question: "Am I in actual danger?" Often, the answer is an almost comically clear "no!".

So fear not only stops us from presenting unconventional ideas in environments with a lack of psychological safety – which is what we most often consider and read about when it comes to creativity and innovation – it even stops us from accessing *our own brain's* ability to make interesting connections in the first place.

Why is it that the brain fears its own creativity? After all, what is contained in our heads, ie. ideas we keep to ourselves, cannot threaten our social status in the way that we imagine a public address could. I have not yet found a good, exhaustive evidence-based answer to this mystery, but I have a theory: consistency bias.

Once we have made a decision, we start to look for confirmations that we made the right choice. This behaviour is driven by what is referred to as consistency bias; a strong tendency and desire to stick with the decisions that we have made, rather than changing course, which, again, saves energy for the brain.

If you are not already a highly creative person, trying to access your innate ability to form great ideas is an inconsistency. As you actively explore this inconsistent behaviour, your amygdala will experience difficulty in making predictions about dangers, because such dangers may lurk in unknown (or at least unusual) territory.

But due to the way that the brain processes this type of information and communicates with your nervous system, it never signals: "hmmm, this is hard to predict, could it be dangerous?". All you will ever get is: "Danger!", as previously discussed, albeit at various volumes.

When this happens, we feel anxious, and move quickly to a stressed state of mind, where cortisol and focused thinking effectively blocks our creativity. This, in turn, leads to a vicious cycle, since we now receive even more confirmation that we are not creative, and the consistency of that self-image is not merely preserved, but even reinforced.

It is essential to overcome such fear, and all other reasons why you might feel anxious and stressed, in order to find your most creative self. It is not a matter of wellbeing as much as it is a matter of vital access to the brain's *functions* that drive creativity, such as diffused thinking. The saying that cortisol cuts off functions in your brain and body, centering all of your focus on fight, flight or freeze, is not a figure of speech but an actual neurological block. When you fear, you are locked out.

The anxiety and fear of changing yourself and your self-image, or to present your ideas to other people for that matter, can be dealt with in the manner of any other fear. The best way to overcome them is to face them, or, to act as if. So to 'try and fail' over and over again is not really to fail, but to incrementally conquer new intellectual territory.

Our brains are, as you now know, obsessed with preserving energy, even the hysterical amygdala, and logically it is less costly for the brain to decline to react than it is to trigger a fear response, if there is no real danger. So the secret to overcoming your fear is to actively help your amygdala to recalibrate its prediction of danger, given the relatively safe situation at hand.

"What is the worst that can happen?". The first time that we ask ourselves this question, before we go up on stage to give a speech, or are given a slot to present our idea for the C-suite, we usually feel no effect whatsoever. The anxiety is just as strong after engaging in this attempt to help ourselves, as it was before. But, and this is the key to understanding how 'facing your fear' really works, you actually will experience a positive effect: it comes the next time that you try the same thing!

By no means will you feel completely safe and at ease this next time, but you will feel less anxious and afraid than the previous time, because you have helped the amygdala to better predict the situation as perhaps-not-so-dangerous. As you repeat again: "what is the worst thing that can happen?", you trigger a virtuous cycle. Because, from now on, overcoming your fear is the new normal, the new consistency, and each time you repeat this fear-facing process you confirm to yourself, including your amygdala, that the thing you are doing is not really dangerous.

There is one more important detail that you need to know about this process: you need to imagine... what is the worst thing that could actually happen? And you need to accept that thing as a potential outcome. For this type of fear, you will find that the answer to the question is really quite silly, seen from a life or death perspective. People might laugh at you. Maybe you risk vomiting on the boardroom table. Perhaps even pass out. So what?!

If we change the scene back to feeling anxious about trying to ideate through diffused thinking, the potential answers to the question "what is the worst thing that can happen?" become even more ridiculous. I do not even know what answers to provide as examples! Nonetheless, if you accept whatever adverse outcome that you imagine, I can promise you: that particular thing will not occur.

Yet that feeling of self-doubt may persist because we are testing new territory. Its ugly face has a name, and it is impostor syndrome, as previously discussed. One way to deal with impostor syndrome, ie. self-doubt, is to remember the distinction between reality and perception that I made in part one - that they are two separate things - and then ask yourself this question: "is doubt an aspect of reality or of perception?"

I would argue that this type of doubt is a function of expectations not met by experience, so it is really an aspect of perception. If you can just remember this insight during such times of self-doubt, you stand a good chance of overcoming this limiting emotion. Because with such insight at hand you can divert from unmet expectations by focusing on real progress.

One example would be my own experience writing this book, when I, without much thinking, created expectations for myself to write 5,000 words per week during the fall of 2022. When I failed to deliver this after only two or three weeks, I started to doubt myself. "I do not have what it takes to complete this project," I told myself.

But an assessment of the actual words written, rather than the word-count, revealed new material that I felt really proud of! Laying the expectations aside, and the related perception of being an author-impostor, allowed me to focus on the reality of the situation. It is the classical glass half-full rather than half-empty mindshift trick.

The big culprit, as we explore creative thinking, is time, and timing, on which almost all of our expectations depend. "I expect to finish this project on time", or "we expect to close the deal within two weeks" are other examples that come to mind. This kind of thinking does not work for ideation, or creative work in general, at least not the kind explored in this book. Instead, make sure you are having fun learning, and take all the time that you need!

Speaking of time, there is a wonderful method for achieving long-term goals, known as 'delayed gratification', which works for everything from becoming a better leader to quitting smoking. Its core principle is to delay whatever counter-constructive treat you want to give yourself by some measure of time, and this process will deliver your long-term goal.

A great example is if you want to quit smoking, but feel you should treat yourself to a cigarette. If you are able to tell yourself "yes, I will have a smoke, but in ten minutes", your brain will accept the treat as already given, instantly release dopamine, and ten minutes later you will no longer feel the need to light up that cigarette.

I find that this approach is also a great way of dealing with doubt when you cannot find a specific reason for why you feel it, even though I am not aware of any study that has tested 'delayed acknowledgement' on feelings of self-doubt. Usually, the time-unit I use is one day, so when doubt creeps up on me, I try to pause, take a deep breath, and say to myself: "okay, I will succumb to this doubt, tomorrow". And then I try to continue with something simple and fun.

When tomorrow comes, the continued creative exploration that I'm engaging in (while acting as if there is nothing to doubt) has often progressed beyond the need for self-doubt, so the whole thing has become a non-issue. If the feeling of doubt persists, I repeat the process, but ensure that I get a good night's sleep. Most of the time, this simple process resolves all, and any, clouding in my thinking.

Before moving on, I should state here that research on the effect of our moods and emotions on creative thinking is somewhat unbalanced. There is an abundance of studies linking positive psychology to increases in creative ability, but far fewer studies have investigated the effects of negative psychology on creative thinking, and these latter studies also indicate ambiguous results. Therefore, since a positive attitude clearly seems to yield good results in terms of creative thinking, I try to fully embrace that state of mind.

A habit you should adopt: let go of fear, and develop a positive mindset in general. You may think that is easy to say and hard to do, but, in fact, hordes of people achieve this all the time, and you can too!

Cultivate curiosity

Curiosity serves at least two purposes for the creative thinker.

Firstly, it makes it a lot easier, and more fun, to collect random knowledge; ie. the dots that you may eventually connect to form a great new idea.

Secondly, research has shown that individuals who cultivate their curiosity are less susceptible to confirmation bias; thus, they naturally have a bigger thinking box than less curious people.

Both of these values are beautifully captured in a statement by Daniel J. Boorstin, who once said: "The greatest obstacle to discovery is not ignorance—it is the illusion of knowledge." (Sometimes attributed to Stephen Hawking, but the original source appears to be Boorstin).

What we think we know limits our learning explorations,

as well as our ability to think outside the box. So a good start to cultivating curiosity is to adopt a core intellectual principle: that all knowledge is approximate, temporary, and subject to change at any time. Or in a shorter format: do not be certain about any of your knowledge. This may sound like a very depressing principle, especially for the expert, but can in fact be a source of great joy once accepted.

For example, let us say that you are an expert in bicycle design. You naturally believe that you know how bikes are built. But did you know that a few cycle brands build their frames with bamboo? How is that bamboo grown, and where?

One company that specialises in this is based out of Ghana, where they use both wild bamboo and material from plantations. Is that sustainable? Do they buy FSC-approved (Forest Stewardship Council) bamboo to build their bikes? No, they do not, because there is no FSC-certified bamboo anywhere in the world. How can that be?

Well, bamboo is a grass, not a tree, hence not classified as wood, and therefore not monitored by the FSC. Chances are that when you first saw a bamboo-bike on this learning path, you thought something like: "Ha! A bike made of wood!". But it is really made from grass. So how much do you really know about how to build a bike?

You can imagine this method to cultivate curiosity as walking to the edge of one of your inner forest monocultures - in the example above, the trees related to bike building - and from there adding new trees that do not remotely resemble the previous ones. In short, you start to cultivate the rainforest in your mind, not from an empty patch, but from a familiar place that is easily accessible to you. Gradually, you will 'uncivilise' your inner forest, and find yourself far away from the original monoculture from which you began your exploration.

There are three principles to follow in order to conduct this kind of exploration well, particularly if your goal is to not merely gain raw material for future ideation, but to stimulate your natural tendency to be curious.

Firstly, allow for this process to take up considerable amounts of time. Life-hacks to incorporate learning in your busy everyday life can be helpful, but are seldom adequate in my experience. Schedule time to learn random stuff, and allow yourself to get lost in new interesting experiences and knowledge, as you encounter them.

Secondly, make sure you are engaged in active learning. I am not the kind of person that will say things like "audio books do not work", or "YouTube will make you dumb". But to passively 'hear' rather than 'listen to' an audiobook, or to watch some documentary without reflecting on its content, will not give you the insight that you need. Remember, to explore the intricacies of any subject is to create many connectors for that subject, which will help you make stronger and more unique connections in the future.

Thirdly, follow your lust and intuition from one subject to the next. In fact this is *key* to really nurture your curiosity - your passion for learning and questioning what you, and anyone really, knows about anything. One could argue that there are two implicit rules embedded in this third principle: never try to find 'useful' new knowledge for your inner rainforest, you can only know in hindsight what became useful anyway; and never exclude any type of learning that you feel inclined to explore, not even stuff that you think you already know.

Creating an inner rainforest in your mind is supposed to be messy. If you worry about the direction and usefulness of new trees, it means that you are trying to optimise and be efficient, which will have an adverse effect on your creativity.

That is why, in this particular case, it makes perfect sense to follow your passion. Remember, passion is a lousy compass but great fuel, and what you really need on your life-long learning journey is, indeed, fuel. And when you occasionally run out of fuel, conviction that this method is your best foundation for future glory will help you cross the chasm.

A habit you should adopt: Make time for random learning in your schedule. 20 minutes every morning, or three hours spread out over three different days of the week, or every Sunday from sunrise to sunset. Whatever works for you. Make sure this learning is fun, follow your curiosity, and let go of all 'judgement' regarding usefulness of the information that you indulge!

Routinely zone out

In my experience, using our brain's innate ability to form interesting ideas during diffused thinking is one of the most underutilised methods in modern creative business practices. There are tons of books available on using Design Thinking and workshop facilitation to create new ideas, and how to apply all kinds of logic to generate innovative solutions. And all of these things can be useful, and sometimes even generate great ideas. But they all require us to focus, or they put us into contexts where we are effectively unable to zone out, and consequently are unable to slide into diffused thinking mode.

For example, knowing what you now know, consider once again brainstorming sessions in conference rooms - full of colourful sticky notes, coffee, and enthusiastic people. Everyone in that room will have a brain either full of dopamine or cortisol, which makes them either able to learn and focus on logical problems (the ranger follows a plan), or unlikely to perform any kind of useful intellectual task due to fear. Magically connecting dots, half-consciously, is just not going to happen in that room! That is why 'creative' meetings such as this should be facilitated around *exploring the problem* at hand; sharing dots, rather than generating ideas.

In my view, ideas are, by definition, the product of a single mind, just as a DJ's mix is created by that DJ's hands alone. Because the dots exist inside your head, and the connections between them happen there alone. Regardless of this, teams ideating together can be incredibly effective, and can conceive ideas that no single person would have generated. But what that really represents is a compounded series of ideas that created new dots and connections in the heads of those people. Still, all the components of the final idea have their origins inside individual brains.

Therefore, we must focus on you and your own mind to create the best possible conditions for ideal ideation, even if you are part of a great team. Improving your grasp of ideation will benefit not just yourself, but your entire team.

Mastering diffused thinking is a gift that never stops giving, but many people never deliberately explore this mystical state of their minds. In many ways, this makes perfect sense.

For example, how many of your responsibilities at work leave room for you to perform without any focus or plan? How interested are your spouse or your kids when you are totally zoned out, and don't pay any attention to them? These are rhetorical questions, as we can all recognise that there are practical barriers in the way of our opportunity and ability to engage in diffused thinking.

Yet diffused thinking is essential for our mental wellbeing, and is closely related to the important work done by the brain during REM (rapid eye movement) sleep. Or, for that matter, rest and sleep in general, really. In accordance with this, you should start a habit of 'zoning out' more often.

Just to be clear, to 'zone out' does not mean taking any substances, or doing anything illegal or immoral, but simply to completely relinquish mental focus and direction. The following passage provides some things that you can do to stimulate the process of seeping into a state of diffused thinking.

Be alone without stimuli - no screens, no books, no music, or speech. Stare at the ceiling, or at a fire in your fireplace, or at the wind in the leaves outside your window. Try to pay attention to your peripheral field of view, and the low noise in your environment. Do not focus hard on these things, just divert your attention away from your focal point, and the voice-pitch spectrum. Now let your mind wander, and gently observe what happens.

Take a walk in a forest or an empty park. You should make sure not to take a fast, exercise-like walk, but instead a rather slow and lazy one; light movement like this also stimulates diffused thinking in general. Try to do the same things as in the previous example here - do not focus on what you see down the path that you are walking on; instead let your attention rest in your blurry peripheral vision. And do not tune in to the birds singing, rather drench your thoughts in the soft noise emanating from the wind in the canopy above.

Take a long shower in medium-hot water; ie. a temperature that will not call on your attention and focus. Almost everyone has experienced 'eureka moments' in the shower at some point. This is likely related to the fact that showers generate a lot of white noise, sound without specific tone, as discussed previously. After a relatively short while, this white noise will have overwhelmed our brain's attempts to distinguish any useful cognitive information, and we will lose all focus as a result. When this happens, the ranger sees its chance, and goes for a random walk in the mental forest it is nurturing, and, voilá, new ideas are born!

If you, like me, have decided that a constant stream of new ideas is essential for your sanity as well as for your career, you should schedule recurring 'zone out' time, several times a week. There are, of course, an infinite number of ways to help your brain float; those suggested here are just a few classic examples. When you plan your zone out sessions, you should have the following concepts and ideas in mind.

Firstly, social contact will almost certainly pull your brain into focused thinking mode, because you will give it a plan to behave according to social norms. Nikola Tesla once insightfully stated in a *New York Times* interview: "Originality thrives in seclusion free of outside influences beating upon us to cripple the creative mind. Be alone, that is the secret of invention; be alone, that is when ideas are born."

Secondly, make sure you are not exposed to physical conditions that risk calling on your attention, because that too will force you to focus and make a plan to fix whatever it is that bothers you. I offered the example above with medium-hot water in the shower, but the same applies to how you, for example, are dressed on your walk. Freezing is not a good way to relax your mind, nor is being hungry or thirsty.

And regarding the pace of walking, you may also conclude that you might as well get some exercise while you are out trying to be creative. That is a plan, right? So skip the exercise and just go for a zone out. Anything that calls for your attention in the physical domain is bad for getting into a state of float. You should try to be on autopilot.

Because of what I just stated regarding exercise, it is worth noting that some people get their best ideas during quite intense physical activity, such as running for hours. That is because, for them, that activity has become a reference point for the brain, enabling it to turn on the autopilot. Thus, attention-seeking due to physical conditions is very individual, and relative to that which our bodies and minds are accustomed to being subjected. But the general rule is to take it easy.

Thirdly, and this is the more general and abstract rule:

understand that your brain is constantly giving itself a plan to predict what is going on around you. Our minds are obsessed with making sense of things in our environment, mostly to cater for our basic needs, such as physical and social security. Whatever you can do to shut down such prediction processes will help to induce a state of diffused thinking. These processes are, of course, all connected to our senses, which are constantly probing the outside world, so you can design sensory experiences that impact them.

In my experience, which aligns with much of the research in this area, there are two main strategies to effectively disrupt the brain's focus to predict what is going to happen next. The first is to remove all of the sensory sources that may call upon the brain to make a prediction about the imminent future; that is, to remove sounds and sights that may disturb you. Staring at the ceiling is a classic example of this, or lying in bed in the evening and getting a killer idea, just as you were about to fall asleep.

The other strategy, which I myself generally find more useful, is to overwhelm the senses with signals that are so idiosyncratic and dominating that the brain soon gives up on trying to make sense of them. This is another effect of the brain's obsessions with saving energy; its laziness. The white noise in the shower is a classic example here, but there are other ways that you can explore as well.

Two of my favourite vision overwhelming exercises use fractionalised sunlight to turn off the brain's focus on making sense of sight. One is to sit by the ocean, and watch the sun glitter in the water; the other is to lay on my back in a large bird's-nest swing that I have hung up in the forest where I live, and watch the sun shine through the countless leaves in the canopy above me. As I explained previously, direct your sensory input to the peripheral, and your brain will soon give up on trying to make sense of what it is seeing.

Music can also be an incredibly effective way of shutting down your brain's prediction processes. Personally, I find all kinds of vocal music impossible to use, except maybe large choirs using few hard consonants. But repetitive, ambient, low-pitch music at a moderate volume can be great to both shut out noise from your surroundings, and to drown your inner dialogue (if you have one, I have about three or four at any given time...); both of which may prevent you from losing focus.

An interesting observation is that the same technique can also be applied to induce a state of flow, rather than a state of float. I have been experimenting with 'alpha brain wave' sounds that are supposed to stimulate diffused thinking, but have not found any additional effect, personally, compared to monotone music.

Finally, the same two strategies further apply to your bodily experience. To not feel any specific physical sensation at all is one way to stop the brain from making predictions that call for your attention. But this sense can also be effectively overwhelmed, with a loss of focus typically resulting.

Personally, I think light massage in a massage chair can have this effect, or sitting alone in a bubble bath.

Generally speaking, though, seeing and hearing are the two most important neural prediction processes to 'disrupt', in order to zone out and let the mind wander for longer periods of time.

A habit you should adopt: Schedule time to relax your mind and learn how to get into a state of float. Find your own rhythm and need for time to do this well. If creative thinking is part of your work, make sure you classify all thinking modes as work, even (or perhaps especially) the diffused mode of thinking.

Develop mindsight

Just as the chapter "How to catch ideas" was the most difficult to write for part two of this book, this chapter, that deals with the development of a habit to do just that, was equally demanding to deliver in a clear and concise fashion. However, for the past couple of years I have practised the habit of *Mindsight* (Bantam, 2009), which is not just an effective method, but also the title of a great book by Daniel J. Siegel.

Thanks to Siegel's work and words in *Mindsight*, I think I have been able to convey this incredibly abstract concept into something understandable and useful. His book is not at all about ideation, innovation or creativity, but it teaches a mental model, referred to by the author as 'mindsight', that I have found to be a great tool for catching ideas!

Essentially, mindsight is a lot like mindfulness meditation

- observe your mind and your thoughts without judgement. Simply look at the stream of thoughts flowing through your mind, without trying to navigate and steer them. When you observe the workings of your mind, it enables you to realise that you are *not* your mind; it is just a machine that is part of you, and you can decide what to do with its output.

However, mindsight and mindfulness meditation are generally practised for reasons other than to boost ideation. These are techniques utilised to provide relief from stress and anxiety, while also providing other mental health benefits. Mindfulness is all about observing your mind in the present, and being at peace with whatever it cooks up. Mindsight, however, goes a step further, and aims to construct a mind-monitoring model that can also include modifiers; ie. strategies to change certain thinking patterns.

Mindsight can therefore be used as a tool to more consciously observe the brain working in diffused mode, as well as to catch and stop it when it is trying to box you in. The key idea in mindsight practice is to use focus to actively see and change how we think and feel. This presents a tricky dichotomy for using mindsight to observe the brain working in diffused mode, since we know that the brain is either in focused mode, or in diffused mode, at any given time.

However, I have found that as I practise the observation of thought in real time, ie. mindsight, it is possible to be both focused and diffused simultaneously. The trick to make it work is in how you blend them. As discussed previously, it is virtually impossible to partially activate the diffused mode of thinking while you are in focused mode. The executive control network, that is highly active during focused thinking, simply dominates your consciousness too much for such partial activation of diffused mode to be possible.

The opposite is, however, possible as long as the scope of the focus is very limited. That is, it is possible to zone out and let diffused mode of thinking take over, while maintaining a small window of focus; just enough to observe what is going on. Think of it as quietly monitoring the ranger from a satellite in the sky above the forest. Or recall the psychoanalyst analogy from part two of this book.

The advantages of being able to do this are numerous. The most obvious benefit is that you will consciously observe many more interesting ideas than if you rely solely on your diffused mode brain to bring them to the surface. Another skill that you will potentially develop is the ability to influence your thought process even in diffused mode; for example, to delay switching to focused mode as some exciting idea forms.

Think about what happens in the shower, or just before sleep when an idea 'comes to you'; it grabs your attention, your focus, which is great because that makes you remember it, but it also ends your diffused exploration, and the 'unboxed' emergence of that idea.

A third benefit is that it will become increasingly easy to deliberately switch to the diffused mode of thinking; ie. to float. People that can daydream on purpose, influence the experience as it unfolds, and then remember it afterwards - essentially what Carl Jung called 'active imagination' - have mastered exactly this skill. This is very much how I imagine Joanne Rowling on that delayed train from Manchester to London.

Teaching this specific mindsight technique is about as simple and straightforward as teaching another DJ how to do a scratch mix - all you will ever get is a pointer in the right direction. But you need to discover and practise this technique yourself, in order to develop your own personal touch and skill. Here is how I would recommend getting started.

Firstly, discover ways to more or less predictably switch from focused to diffused mode of thought. It is important to unwind and zone out to achieve this. Absolutely do not try to steer yourself in a specific direction; I think that is the most common mistake. Often people have a need to come up with a solution to some specific problem, which, of course, creates focus and a mind with a plan.

Ditch the plan. Try walking slowly in an environment with few distractions, such as a forest. Take a bath. Laying down and staring at the ceiling may work, although light movement, saltwater-floating, and other similar phenomena, are known stimuli for diffused thinking. Personally, I prefer walking in a forest.

Secondly, try a typical mindfulness approach to be more

present during sessions of diffused thinking. The important thing is to learn to only observe and not interfere. The moment that you start thinking: "ha! That is an interesting idea! What if..." you will create focus and a plan, and there is a big risk that you will bring yourself out of the session, and the subconscious emergence of perhaps an even bigger idea.

On the one hand, ending the session may be exactly what you want, since your brain has made an interesting connection that you wish to bring up to the surface. On the other hand, right now you are still exploring and learning, and you need to develop discipline, so that you can venture deeper and deeper into your own consciousness.

Thirdly, start writing down retrospectives of your sessions; whatever you can remember, regardless of how silly or useless it may appear in the moment. This will likely interfere with the process at first, because when you decide to take notes you will have a plan to remember and document your thoughts, and, consequently, you may find yourself becoming too focused, which will detract from the process.

I have found that the best way to deal with this problem is to always have a notebook at hand, and rather than plan for taking notes during specific sessions, I just do it whenever I naturally slip into a diffused mode of thought, and come out of it again with something interesting that I can document.

What you observe or remember is not important, nor is what we perceive as quality important. Remember, you are exploring and learning. If your brain connects fermented herring with fried banana, or suggests using butter instead of rubber as tyres on your car, that is just fine. (Well, perhaps not in practice...) But, eventually, something completely brilliant will pop up, and you want to be there to catch it!

The more straightforward way to use mindsight is to observe your thought process in focused mode; in the process spotting thinking errors and biases. For this type of monitoring of the mind, I really like the 'mind within the mind' model, with a spatial reference inside the head. For example, you imagine that you have a second brain within your brain that is located just behind your forehead, where you would imagine that a third 'all-seeing eye' would be present if you had one.

This second brain is only an observer and analyst. It has no feelings, no control of any bodily functions, nor anything of that nature. But you can use it to 'see' how you think. You can also use it to ask fundamental questions about what your core mind is doing.

I find this method very hard to practise unless that second brain is given its own hypothetical (yet *very* specific) physical location in my head. But once that location has been established as a mind within the mind, I can focus on it to observe my own thought process, and call out at least some of my brain's bullshit, shortcuts, and restrictive box-ins.

This mind within the mind is essentially the psychoanalyst that I described in part two of this book, at work. But, of course, the implementation of this seventh sense, as Siegel calls it, is not through classical psychoanalysis questions, quietly asked inside your head, but instead through the practise of mindsight.

If you believe that this habit, although 'illusive' and 'fluffy', could be the most valuable of all the habits that I propose for you in the overall mastering of *The Ideation Equation*, I highly recommend reading the book *Mindsight* yourself. If you, on the other hand, are more curious than totally convinced, an online search will be highly productive in terms of learning and experimenting with this, as well as accessing other mind-observing techniques.

A habit you should adopt: Experiment with meditation techniques such as Mindsight or mindfulness. Familiarise yourself with your own mind from a detached position within the mind, and routinely think about how and what you think.

Practise idea recycling

One of the most interesting and productive innovators of our time is Bill Gross, the founder of Idealab, and father of at least 150 tech companies. In his 2015 address at the TED conference, Gross presented data collected throughout his career on what made some ideas more successful than others.

It's interesting to note then that the single most important factor in his dataset was timing. It was not that ideas turned out to be 'bad', or too expensive to realise, or that he was unable to assemble the right teams to execute them. No, most of the time when things did not work out it was because the timing was wrong. In the case of Gross, he was probably mostly too early, but occasionally he must also have been too late.

This insight, which is not entirely anecdotal evidence,

since Gross had two decades of data behind his findings, backs up a principle about ideation and innovation that many creators have practised throughout history, from Archimedes to Gross: never throw away ideas! At least, not ideas that cannot immediately be assessed as either good or bad. But even ideas that have features that can immediately be labelled as 'bad' are often valuable starting points for other ideas.

However, idea recycling can be a practice that is easier said than done, precisely because ideas that are ahead of their time by many years, or perhaps even decades, are easily forgotten. I have three methods, or systems, for ideas with different features, that I find effective. Hopefully, these can inspire you to set up your own idea recycling ecosystem.

System one: ideas that I cannot put into any particular short-term context, or are obviously much too early, I simply place in my digital calendar as recurring events every six or twelve months, forever. This ensures that my calendar provides me with constant reminders of old ideas that I still have not used.

Sometimes I change these ideas for the next reminder, and some of these ideas have been on my calendar for more than ten years, changing in this time on five or six separate occasions. But over these years, I have also been inspired by them, and have 'recycled' them into new ideas that have benefitted my business in various ways. Why use a standard digital calendar, and not some fancy idea management system? Because the calendar is integrated into my daily life, easy to use, and free.

System two: ideas that have a strong portion of identity built into them, which is often the case for me with ideas for consumer products or services, I usually give a name, while also buying a corresponding domain name. This becomes a yearly reminder to do something with the idea, every time the renewal fee is due.

The cost associated with renewing domains for these very 'tangible' ideas is a feature, not a drawback, because it forces me to think through what the idea is about, and if the right time is likely to come or not. If I fail to address this then I will simply feel like a sucker who is just wasting money on useless domain names.

System three: in common with many other creative people, I am a huge fan of note-taking, but, rather than a standard-sized journal, I use a much larger 'idea book', with completely blank pages. This book goes with me almost everywhere, and is used mostly for ideas that I intend to use or explore further in the near future.

Yet many ideas are abandoned on second thought, and my idea books are full of scribbles and sketches for things that sound and look ridiculous in hindsight. However, these books are invaluable when a creative block hits. When I am stuck, and further diffusive thinking renders no results, I always go back to my idea books for inspiration, or a good laugh.

Idea recycling also helps innovators to achieve quality through quantity. It is a widely accepted fact that the most predictable path to a great idea is to have many ideas. A few years ago, I had the chance to sit down and talk over dinner with Allen Morgan - the managing director of Idealab. Given this rare opportunity, I asked him what it was like to run an operation that realised *all* of Bill Gross' ideas.

His response was along the lines that Gross generated more ideas than anyone could handle, but also that the high volume of ideas gave them a lot to choose from, and that many ideas shared core components with each other, or borrowed features from otherwise abandoned ideas. So it's important to emphasise that just because an idea appears poor or useless in the short-term, it does not mean that it will not have some value in the future; value that may not be immediately clear in the present.

Lastly on this topic, idea documentation and recycling are also valuable as important sources of learning. In common with any other piece of information, your ideas turn into trees in your inner forest. Many such trees will form a magnificent rainforest where evolution can have its way, and yield much more interesting results than in your monocultures.

So the more ideas that you manage to conceive, acquire, internalise, and recycle, as well as actively recalling every now and then, the better the internal environment to nurture new ideas becomes. It is a virtuous cycle that you can and should use to your advantage.

A habit you should adopt: Get an idea-book or a journal and start documenting *all* of your ideas. Or start using your calendar or some other piece of information technology that is already part of your daily life. Realise and recognise that you are free to reuse your ideas as many times, and in as many variations, as you choose.

Design
thought-experiments

The problem with trying to give advice for how to expand your thinking box is that there are so many beliefs, heuristics and biases, in addition to the few common ones I have mentioned in this book, that there are literally as many different boxes as there are people. To say "do this specific thing" would be similar to a doctor providing treatment advice to a group of undiagnosed patients. Not a wise thing to do...

However, as with physical wellness and fitness, there are general things that you can do to improve your thinking processes. As I have previously declared, this book is not about the fundamentals of mental health, which, by the way, are physical activity, balanced nutrition, and good (more!) sleep. But are there, perhaps, other general advice for thinking-box-expanding habits?

I would like to think that there are, and the habit that I find most interesting, useful, fun, challenging, but also generalisable, is to regularly design thought-experiments. Such an experiment only takes place inside your head, and is fundamentally different from most real-world experiments in terms of how the underlying hypothesis is devised. Traditional science is generally occupied with asking *why* things are the way they are. Good thought-experiments, on the other hand, ask *what if* something was a certain way.

Of course, 'real science' can conduct experiments based on *what if* hypotheses as well, but in contrast to the thought-experiment, it must then be possible for such experiments to be carried out. Inside your head, that is not a limitation you need to take into account.

The most famous example of a thought-experiment, that broke thinking barriers, and led to a groundbreaking new idea, is probably Einstein's design of a what-if-travelling-experience at the speed of light. He reasoned along the lines of "what if I could travel at the speed of light, alongside a light beam and observe it?". From this perspective, Einstein was able to see that what he would then be able to observe could not be explained by Maxwell's equations, which constituted a rigid thinking-barrier for physicists at the time.

This anomaly led him, eventually, to his theory of special relativity, which is the physics-thinking-box we are still trapped in today. Perhaps that is because it is a perfect theory - a mental model that precisely describes the real world.

One may think that the example above is a one-off lucky shot, but Einstein, in fact, designed numerous thought-experiments involving imaginary trains, elevators in space, and painters falling off the roof of a house. And then there is Schrödinger's cat, which I am sure you have, at least, heard mentioned previously, and the 'trolley-problem', usually involving a trolley heading down a track, with a bunch of kids standing on it, a lever to switch tracks, and an old lady on the other track. Will you pull the leaver and save the kids, but kill the old lady?

Thought-experiments are something that you should start designing for fun, but that can eventually have profound effects on your ability to think 'usefully' outside the box. Start with something easy. "What if I was immortal, what would I do tomorrow afternoon?" Or engage in a thought-experiment where you change places with someone. Such thought-experiments have rendered a few good movies, of which *The Hot Chick* (Touchstone/Disney 2003) is my favourite so far.

Once you start to get a hang of it, pick topics that will truly mess with your most well-established beliefs. At the time of writing, I am myself exploring a thought-experiment, which questions my strong belief in science. "What if the scientific method was disproven as the best way to figure out how the world works?" How could that happen? What could disprove science, since proof is itself part of the scientific method? Does such a paradox hint at some extraordinary insight, or is it just an intellectual distraction, also known as mumbo-jumbo?

A good principle when designing more challenging thought-experiments is to put something 'impossible' as a central concept. Meaning that, "what if I was the CEO", *as an example,* is not a very challenging idea to explore, even if it may be tempting.

Let us use this example as a sign that you want to explore management principles at your workplace. Then, instead, ask yourself something along the lines of "what if all companies were democracies?", or perhaps "what if becoming a CEO meant one only had 3 years left to live?", or something else that 'makes no sense', but nonetheless forces you to think in a much-expanded box, or perhaps even an entirely different box than the one within which you are currently trapped.

Thought-experiments are also good mental training for the ideator, since they can be explored in both focused and diffused modes of thinking. Generally, exploring the implications of logic, and the direct consequences of the *what if* question, are good places to start. That sounds like a plan, so you should do that in focused mode.

But then, as you enter a state of float, try to gently help your mind daydream about what it would be like to live in the world that you have created. If Einstein explored the mathematical implications of observing a ray of light at the speed of light in a state of flow, he likely experienced the imaginary beauty and strangeness of that situation in a later state of float.

A habit you should adopt: Routinely design thought-experiments that force you to challenge your beliefs and common ways of reasoning. Explore these models with both focused and diffused thinking.

Hang out with other creative thinkers

Daniel has pointed out something to me during the last couple of years, as he has been learning bits and pieces of *The Ideation Equation* and gradually becoming a more creative thinker; that it is an alienating skill to possess. To me, this was not news, but rather something that I have experienced my entire life, more or less. Several of my friends, who have given me invaluable feedback on this work, have expressed similar experiences.

In fairness, the amygdala has a point when it tries to make us scared of our own creativity. Because it can be lonely to be the only person in a tribe thinking outside of the shared box, and in ancient times that alienation could probably kill you during times of trouble. I do not believe that loneliness is inevitable for the creative genius, but I think it is a fairly common price that people pay for being different.

Today, I am not at all a lonely person, although I have to admit that I have quite few close friends, and I enjoy being alone with my thoughts immensely. But I also do not think I am very well understood by most people around me, with the exception of my closest family and friends. That they get me is, of course, due mostly to selection bias but also due to the social proximity effect. If you buy a Picasso painting because you like it, and then stare at it for long enough, you will probably understand its deeper meaning.

Did this author just compare himself to a Picasso painting?!

This chapter begins and ends with its core message, to find some new friends as you become an increasingly creative person, which, as previously discussed, triggers a virtuous cycle that will spur even more creativity. But in order to pick them well, it may be a good idea to first think about what makes us aliens in our tribes, as creative thinkers.

Firstly, I believe that creative people are both consciously and subconsciously linked to the concept of change in other people's minds. Or, inversely associated with the status quo, would be another way to put it. That could mean that people's amygdalas are, on average, more alert around creative people (because change is unpredictable), which would in turn mean higher levels of cortisol in their brains and bodies.

Secondly, I can only reason from my own experience, but

from that perspective I suspect that highly creative people are more often regarded as threats to other people. By that I do not mean physically threatening, but a threat to the social status or position held by other people. Again, I think this is mostly a subconscious reaction, a residual instinct from when we lived on the savanna. But then there have also been times in my life when people have bluntly told me that they do feel threatened by my ability to think outside the box.

In fact, this tendency often goes even deeper than this. Thinking which is outside of the usual accepted parameters is deeply troublesome to many people, precisely because it threatens to disturb the box of comfort within which they reside.

One of the most memorable lines in any cinematic feature film comes from *A Few Good Men,* in which Jack Nicholson's character derisively notes that Tom Cruise's character "can't handle the truth". In many cases, this applies broadly to the human race. Many people simply do not want to know the whole truth, as they have achieved a state of comfort with the status quo, and the truth could potentially shatter this.

As a free thinker, you are, therefore, continually threatening their comfort! It must also be emphasised that even the most creative thinkers among us are certainly not immune from this innate habit, and this is one of the many reasons why cultivating the mindset and processes associated with free thinking and ideation is so important.

Thirdly, the above experience is closely linked to other

people's perception of creative thinkers being arrogant and self-centred. This is actually not hard to understand. A person who time and again is thinking in a much larger box than their peers is either forced to say "you need to think like me to understand", or to shut up and mind their own business. Both these options can come across as arrogant and self-centred. Of course, there are also creative geniuses who truly are arrogant pricks!

And, fourthly, highly creative thinkers are also often very resourceful and independent. As such, perhaps we do not signal a need for friendship as much as the average person? Many relationships in life are based on different types of codependency, and as you become more independent through your growing creative thinking ability, you may lose the foundation for some of your relationships, as well as for similar new ones.

With these four issues in mind, try to make some new friends. What kind of person would fall outside of these four categories? Well, other creative thinkers, of course! It is not exactly rocket science! In my own experience, it is not that hard to find other free-thinking people, but much harder to change your self-perception about who you hang out with.

I once befriended a very creative person, who I think was grateful for our connection, but that just could not stop commenting about me 'living in the wrong neighbourhood'. It obviously hurt their identity to hang out with someone living 'on the wrong side of town', with their kids in 'the wrong school', and so on. Eventually, we stopped hanging out; it just became too awkward.

I have no doubt that I have been that uncomfortable and somewhat annoying person myself in some other relationship, and most probably you have too. But as creative thinkers, we need to broaden our views of who we become friends with. People like colleagues and industry peers, neighbours, the parents of our kids' friends, or our old classmates for that matter, are classical social contexts where 'normal' people find friends.

But you may also want to try to meet people at the local inventor's association, a writer's café downtown, or join an improv club. The trick is to make creative thinking the central theme for making new friends, not your profession, location, social context, or any other typical demographic. You may even want to launch or join a startup, which is a great way to make new friends (it is how I met Daniel), but that often requires a quite substantial lifestyle change.

A habit you should adopt: Find new contexts where you can make friends with other highly creative people. Do not care so much about what they do, live, like, etc., but focus more about how they can inspire your thinking, and in other ways bring meaning into your life.

Conclusion

The Ideation Equation is an attempt to map out a neuro-natural path to becoming consistently good at conceiving new and exciting ideas, by applying contemporary insights in neuroscience to a practitioner's experience of ideation. Specifically, my own experience of working with innovation and creative problem solving for more than two decades.

As stated in the introduction to this book, it is therefore best to consider this construct of various mental models, thinking modes, and creator habits to build momentum and success, as my opinion of the matter, rather than universal truth. However, I can confidently say that there is more than enough generalisable advice in this book to help anyone become a more creative thinker.

The process to adopt *The Ideation Equation* entails, for most people, a good portion of unlearning old 'truths', and reflecting over why their current thinking style has been configured in its existing form, which was examined in the first part of the book. Then, in part two, you learnt more about how ideation naturally works in the human brain, as well as examining the five activities, or factors, of *The Ideation Equation*. This amounts to three long-term strategies:

- to learn all sorts of random things;
- to make use of your brain's innate ability to connect things;
- to capture and make sense of your brain's magic.

And two shorter-term tactics:

- to take control by marinating in a specific challenge;
- to expand your thinking box.

Looking at the ideation process from a chronological perspective, however, shuffles these activities around, and we need to separate the cultivation of skills from their actual, practical use to make sense of this change of order:

- first, you learn all sorts of random things;
- then you take control by marinating in a specific challenge;
- and you expand your thinking box;
- then you make use of your brain's innate ability to connect things;
- and, finally, capture and make sense of your brain's magic.

The reason why this neat chronological order is not the only way, not even the 'default' way, I present these activities is that you need to constantly practise, enhance and use the strategic skills to keep them sharp. You cannot, for example, start to care about your ability to 'zone out' only when you have a specific challenge to deal with, and expect exceptional results. *The Ideation Equation* is a lifestyle, not just another business process.

Although it should be clear to anyone reading this book that it deals solely with improving the ability of a person to conceive ideas, rather than an organisation or group, it recognises that nothing happens in a vacuum. Your emotional relationship with your own ideas, as well as those of your peers, organisations, and communities, on nonconformist thinking, has a profound impact on how successfully you can move from conceiving an idea to implementing it. Which, of course, matters hugely in your everyday life.

In part three of the book, we moved on to address critical habits - changes in behaviour that you can embrace in order to, in time, become a more creative thinker.

Coincidentally, in common with Steven Covey, I believe that there are seven habits of highly creative people, although they mostly differ a lot (but, interestingly, not entirely) from those that Covey outlines in his *Seven Habits of Highly Effective People* (Free Press, 2004).

The habits you should pursue to, eventually, become a creative genius are:

- to let go of fear and negativity;
- to cultivate curiosity;
- to routinely zone out;
- to develop mindsight;
- to practise idea recycling;
- to design thought-experiments;
- to hang out with other creative thinkers.

I was tempted to write "in no particular order" before presenting the above list, but that would not be entirely accurate. To let go of fear, to cultivate curiosity, and to routinely zone out are essential enablers for creative thinking skills, while the other four habits act more as boosters. Put another way, fear may block your creative thinking entirely, while a lack of mindsight might merely make you less effective in collecting all of your ideas.

Likewise, if you fail to cultivate an insatiable curiosity, that constantly drives you down unexpected and completely senseless learning rabbit-holes, you will not acquire enough raw material, dots, to make the connections that could lead to some great ideas. The less diverse the knowledge that you possess, the smaller the probability that you will discover a new idea, a combination of dots, that may change the world.

And that discovery depends, of course, on your ability to look for internal answers, to zone out, and experience the alternate state of consciousness that I call float. If you are struggling with deciding where to start implementing these habits, I suggest you pick this particular habit for two simple reasons: you can get results very quickly, and this habit will soon bring additional positive effects into your life, such as stress relief, and improved concentration when you really need to focus.

Last but not least, I want to thank you for reading *The Ideation Equation*, and I want to ask you for a favour. It would mean a lot to me if you could leave an honest review of this book, on Amazon or wherever it would make sense to you. This is my first book, but perhaps not my last. Just like a DJ, I rely on the response from the audience to make decisions about what sounds to mix in my next creation.

Learning from your experience with this book is the ultimate privilege of being published, as well as having the opportunity to help other people flourish. So please let me and others know what you think of *The Ideation Equation*!

Thank you!

Afterword

By Daniel Borg

As I am writing this, I am pleased to inform you that I am recovering remarkably well from the very serious injuries that I sustained last summer. Doctors expect me to fully recover, and I am in good spirits, eager to share my personal perspectives on *The Ideation Equation*, and creative thinking in general.

In 2020, a senior leader at a multinational corporation asked me to help him communicate his vision and future direction for the organisation. More specifically, he wanted me to create a 'strategic narrative'. For those who are not familiar with the concept, a strategic narrative is a corporate story with a compelling plot, likeable characters, and a climax that plays out five to ten years ahead, articulating and painting a picture of the future that the organisation will aspire to create. The purpose is to incentivise and rally employees around a common and exciting vision of the future that they can understand, emotionally connect with, and work to achieve as a unified collective.

If this leader would have asked me to lead, or even participate in, this visionary process just three years earlier, I would have felt terrified! My physiological response, I am sure, would have been rapidly increasing stress and anxiety levels, causing my heart to race, my palms to sweat, and a sinking feeling in my stomach. I would have felt awful. And I would have declined. Because, back then, writing a strategic narrative would have forced me too far outside of my comfort zone – into the land of creativity.

To understand why, let's briefly examine the essence of writing a strategic narrative.

To begin with, painting a picture of the future, which is what a strategic narrative is supposed to do, requires the creator or creators to envisage many big *and* novel ideas – in other words, expanding the box – using strategic intelligence such as customer research, macro developments, and technology trends as creative inputs.

Generating those ideas also requires an intriguing set of challenges and problems, framed to encourage valuable and novel connections, questions such as: what if drones were powered with solar energy? Wouldn't it be cool if people could capture and deposit atmospheric carbon, similar to how we recycle PET bottles? What would be the consequences of increasing oil-prices on our business model? How might we remove all inconveniences of owning a car?

Then, at some point, creators must select from the generated ideas, and further explore the most interesting directions of the most compelling ones – in other words, interpret and envision different ways that the essence of an idea could manifest itself in the future context of the organisation. In a way, this is about merging the idea, and making it fit with reality. After all, ideas that cannot be realised are of little use, other than for idea-recycling.

Finally, the selected and refined ideas must be coherently organised into an intriguing storyline, with characters, plot, dialogue, set design, climaxes, conflicts and resolutions – basically turned into the manuscript for a short sci-fi movie, or novel.

Doing all of this three years ago would have been impossible due to the analytical-reasoning paradigm that governed my thinking, which prescribed analysis and quantification as the best path to finding solutions. (A paradigm learned during my time at Toyota where I was trained in LEAN, and techniques such as the "5 whys"). To be honest, three years ago I didn't even consider that creativity was a tool in my toolbox, and any creative insights that I had were more like serendipitous moments than the product of consciously harnessing the powers of my creative faculties.

If someone would have told me back then that I would

go on to write several strategic narratives, helping stake out the future for global, multi-billion dollar corporations, I would not have believed them. After all, I didn't consider myself to be a creative person, nor did I appreciate the fun of playing around with ideas and imagination; perhaps due to the perceived inefficient use of time and attention. But this was before I met Linus, and, through his mentoring and collaboration, I learned to harness creativity as a tool to solve complex problems, and create the future.

Today, when I show the strategic narratives that I have created to people, they invariably respond with comments, such as: "I would never be able to write something like that, I am just not creative enough!" or "This is amazing! I wish I was able to create something similar!" And I consistently respond along the lines: "I feel you. A few years ago, I would have said the exact same thing. I was in the same place as you are now; intellectually trapped in the analytical paradigm, doubting my creative capacity and fearing rejection. But through practice and some help from mentors, I have reignited and resumed control of my creative ability, at a level where I can make it work for me, on demand. This transformation is available to you, and anyone else with the willingness to put in the work to develop new habits to revitalise the mind."

Previously, I didn't have a single source of knowledge, nor a particular framework, to which I was able to direct people. A framework that I perceived covered the core habits and routines that collectively enable a professional to practise creativity on demand, and to conceive many big, creative ideas. Thanks to Linus, I now have *The Ideation Equation*.

But just as there are a handful of universal principles to playing soccer well, and many ways of interpreting how to follow them as a player, so there are similar principles for creativity that every aspiring ideator must interpret from their own individual and personal perspective. Those principles have already been discussed previously in the book, so I won't trouble you by repeating them here.

But what I thought might interest readers, and which could also perhaps serve as a source of inspiration, is to briefly describe some aspects of my version of *The Ideation Equation*, and what my personal creative thinking practices look like today, together with some ideas on how to approach the journey. These are not just practices, but key principles that I remind myself of frequently, in order to keep the racing monkey mind focused.

There are six such principles that are core to my creativity practice. The first is to *always be collecting a broad variety of raw material, or 'dots'*. First-hand experience has taught me that my ideaflow – the quality and quantity of my creative output – is directly proportional to the quality and quantity of my inputs. My preferred sources of input are books, podcasts, online newsletters, Google Scholar, documentaries, and thoughtful conversations with other people who are as deeply into collecting dots as I am. And, yes, I do this every day – 365 days a year.

The second is to *generate a lot of ideas for every problem or challenge.* I believe that volume is key. Seldom is the first idea, or ideas, the best that I can come up with. More often, the best idea is a remix or rhyme of another idea or set of ideas, or is sparked by a seemingly unrelated idea.

The third is to *allow, accept and embrace shitty first ideas.* I am told that all good creatives have them! To accept initial crap is how they eventually end up with better ideas, that then can be turned into terrific groundbreaking ideas. My own experience lends support to this claim. Rarely are my best ideas the product of spontaneous inspiration. Rather, they are the product of a consistent refinement process that can last hours, days, weeks, or even years. Without those *shitty first ideas,* I would probably never hatch anything new and interesting.

The fourth is to *reflect and ruminate while walking.* Probably 90% of my ideas, or the insights that then go on to spark new ideas, originate while I'm walking in the forest, ideally along a river or lake, or in old natural forests. The most productive walks in terms of idea generation are when I simultaneously listen to podcasts or audiobooks, or when I take a break from a tough problem. Interestingly, Linus' experience, as described in this book, is that hearing speech generally prevents him from entering float, while for me, sometimes it can actually be helpful during my walks.

The fifth practice is to *constantly and relentlessly capture ideas, dots, questions and insights.* I have realised that my memory is not very reliable when it comes to remembering ideas, facts, connections and insights. Therefore, a keystone habit of my emerging creative practice is to immediately jot down thoughts and ideas as they come to me whenever they are conceived: for example in the shower, while walking or commuting on a bus or train, or while reading a book.

My sixth and final core practice is to *consolidate and connect ideas and insights in Obsidian* – a free software that I use as my personal knowledge management system, or digital library. This is where a lot of the magic happens and where I create exponential leverage. In the Obsidian software, I can create and visualise digital links between every stored piece of information, which enables me to connect, group, and construct new ideas from existing ideas, as well as recycling old ones. Obsidian has been a game-changer for me and I recommend you try it. (Disclaimer: I have no affiliation with Obsidian).

That's the list of my core creative practices and principles, and as you can see they owe a lot to the five key activities, or factors, that make up *The Ideation Equation.*

My journey towards growing my creative abilities hasn't been easy. I can certainly relate to what Linus states in the introduction of this book, that developing your creative skills is comparable to habilitating the muscles on a limb that you have barely used for two decades or more. I have had to learn, or in some cases unlearn and then relearn, many things.

Learning these things has been difficult, yet incredibly interesting. It has been uncomfortable and hard work, but also a lot of fun. It is still uncomfortable to rely on creativity as opposed to analysis, but, thanks to my new creative thinking habits, I am constantly moving closer to a more neutral emotional equilibrium. Yet, all things considered, this journey has required consistency, and learning the skill of emotional labour – the ability to persevere and overcome negative feelings and emotions, especially when things are tough.

Over the years, being a relentless self-learner, I have distilled a handful of principles that I revisit weekly to remind myself that mastery is the product of disciplined and deliberate action that, crucially, must be repeated consistently over long periods of time. Since learning to be more creative is hard, and to help you resist the appeal of quitting during a dip, I thought I would pass some of them along to you, so that you too can use them if you wish:

- **No hurry, no pause.** You can get 95% of the results that you want by calmly putting one foot in front of the other. Remember that velocity is much more important than speed.
- **Slow is smooth.** Smooth is fast. Counterintuitively, doing things carefully, without rushing or cutting corners, and with great precision, will make you go fast.
- **Repetitions create change.** The only thing that creates change is a combination of repetitions and rest. Repetitions to condition, and rest to build the connections.

- **Consistency over intensity.** In the short-term, you are as good as your intensity. In the long-term, you are only as good as your consistency. High intensity is hard to maintain. The key to mastery is consistent practice over long periods of time.

Living in accordance with these principles has brought me immense value, because they have helped me overcome the inevitable dips associated with any learning experience. And I believe that they can help you too.

Before I close this reflection, I want to bring up one last thing that Linus has only briefly touched upon, and which I find paramount to my practice: the importance of what I call *creative collisions*. A creative collision is simply allowing an idea, in some shape or form, to interact with reality, and generate feedback. Because few ideas are born in a perfect eureka moment. With creative collisions, the intent is to let the idea interact with the world, and generate surprising insights that can be added to the process of refining and evolving the idea.

This is contrary to idea testing, where you are validating assumptions about, for example, feasibility, viability or desire; creative collisions, instead, mine the world for signals, surprises and perspectives. The goal is not to seek truth, it is to disrupt the way that you think. A few examples of actions to bring about creative collisions are, bouncing the idea with a thoughtful colleague, building a conceptual prototype and showing it to people, talking to customers about it, viewing every situation from the perspective of the idea, or visiting ground-zero to observe the target audience in action with the idea in mind. This practice is crucial because of our tendency to get stuck in our own heads, and forget about how much the world has to teach us.

Earlier in the book, Linus quoted me saying that leaning on only one thinking style is like being a one-legged man in an ass-kicking contest. Having two legs is not just twice as good as one, it is incomparably better! The same is true in thinking. Being fluent in both the analytical and creative thinking style is not just significantly better; it is more fulfilling and fun too. By shifting your intellectual investments into the development of your creative faculties, I promise you that, in time, you will see magnificent improvements in your ability to creatively solve hard problems, and create the future of your organisation and life.

Although I have been practising and learning core concepts of *The Ideation Equation* for several years already, and have attained a noticeable shift in my level of mastery, I feel as if I am only just getting started. I will continue my journey with the same dedication that I have invested so far. I will seek out work that challenges me to further develop, and hone my awakened creative skills, and I will do so together with other creative thinkers and doers.

On that last note, as Linus transformed his various 'teaching papers' into this book, we made an agreement that if, or rather when, *The Ideation Equation* gets 100 reviews, he and I will begin working together on a joint book project. And since writing a book with Linus fits nicely with how I wish to continue developing my creative abilities, please do me a favour – take a short moment right now, and leave an honest review – let us know what you think of this book! It would mean the world to the both of us.

Thank you! I wish you the best of luck, and much joy, on the continuation of your ideation journey!

Sources and inspirations

Abraham, A. (2018). *The Neuroscience of Creativity.* Cambridge University Press.

Ankersen, R. (2013). *The Gold Mine Effect: Crack the Secrets of High Performance.* Icon Books.

Asghar, R. (2014). *Why Silicon Valley's 'Fail Fast' Mantra Is Just Hype.* Forbes. https://www.forbes.com/sites/robasghar/2014/07/14/why-silicon-valleys-fail-fast-mantra-is-just-hype

Barnett, W. (2016). *Bill Barnett: Where Great Companies – and Leaders – Come From.* Stanford Graduate School of Business on YouTube. https://www.youtube.com/watch?v=PUAuTcdmaAc

Barnett, W. (2021). *Lectures held for LEAD program participants.* Stanford Graduate School of Business LEAD Program.

Boyd, D. & Goldenberg, J. (2013). *Inside the Box: A Proven System of Creativity for Breakthrough Results.* Simon & Schuster.

Bressler, S. & Menon, V. (2010). *Large-scale brain networks in cognition: emerging methods and principles.* Trends in cognitive sciences, 14(6), pp.277-290.

Buckner, R.L. & DiNicola, L.M. (2019). *The brain's default network: updated anatomy, physiology and evolving insights.* Nat Rev Neurosci 20, pp. 593–608.

Burkus, D. (2013). *The Myths of Creativity: The Truth About How Innovative Companies and People Generate Great Ideas.* Jossey-Bass.

Campbell, J. (1991). *The Power of Myth.* Anchor.

Camuffo, A., Cordova, A., Gambardella A. & Spina C. (2019). *A Scientific Approach to Entrepreneurial Decision Making: Evidence from a Randomized Control Trial.* Management Science 66(2): pp. 564-586.

Carlsen, M. & Davidson, M. (2010). *My perfect weekend: Magnus Carlsen.* The Daily Telegraph - 2nd December 2010.

Chivers, T. (2019). *What's next for psychology's embattled field of social priming.* Nature 576, pp. 200-202.

Chown, M. (2021). *Breakthrough: Spectacular stories of scientific discovery from the Higgs particle to black holes.* Faber & Faber.

Collins, J. & Porras, J. (2004). *Built to Last: Successful Habits of Visionary Companies.* HarperCollins Publishers.

Colvin, G. (2010). *Talent is Overrated: What Really Separates World-Class Performers from Everybody Else.* Portfolio.

Covey, S. (2004). *The 7 Habits of Highly Effective People: Powerful Lessons in Personal Change.* Free Press.

Curedale, R. (2019). *Design Thinking Process & Methods; 5th Edition.* Design Community College Inc.

de Bobo, E. (1967). *Lateral Thinking: Be more creative and productive.* Penguin Books.

Dietrich, A. (2002). *Functional neuroanatomy of altered states of consciousness: The transient hypofrontality hypothesis.* Consciousness and Cognition 12 (2003) 231–256.

Dutta, S., Lanvin, B., Rivera León, L. & Wunsch-Vincent, S. (2021). *The Global Innovation Index 2021.* World Intellectual Property Organization

https://www.globalinnovationindex.org/userfiles/file/reportpdf/gii-full-report-2021.pdf

Ericsson, A., Pool, R. (2016). *Peak: Secrets from the New Science of Expertise.* HarperOne.

Fabritius F. & Hagemann, H. (2017). *The Leading Brain: Powerful Science-Based Strategies for Achieving Peak Performance.* TarcherPerigee.

Forbes, B. (1920). *Interview in Forbes Magazine with Thomas Alva Edison.* Forbes.

Godfrey-Smith, P. (2003). *Theory and Reality: An Introduction to the Philosophy of Science (Science and Its Conceptual Foundations series); 1st Edition.* University of Chicago Press.

Gompers, P. *et al.* (2010). Skill vs. Luck in Entrepreneurship and Venture Capital: Evidence from Serial Entrepreneurs. Journal of Financial Economics 96: 18-32.

Grant, A. (2021). *Think Again: The Power of Knowing What You Don't Know.* Viking.

Grant, A. (2016). *Originals: How Non-Conformists Move the World.* Viking.

Gross, B. (2015). *The single biggest reason why start-ups succeed. TED.*

https://www.ted.com/talks/bill_gross_the_single_biggest_reason_why_start_ups_succeed

Johansson, F. (2004). *The Medici Effect: Breakthrough Insights at the Intersection of Ideas, Concepts, and Cultures.* Harvard Business School Press.

Johnson, S. (2011). *Where Good Ideas Come From: The Natural History of Innovation.* Riverhead Books.

Jung, R., Mead, B., Carrasco, J. & Flores, R. (2013). *The structure of creative cognition in the human brain.* Front. Hum. Neurosci. 7:330.

Kahneman, D. (2011). *Thinking, Fast and Slow.* Farrar, Straus and Giroux.

Kitchener, P. & Hales, C. (2022) *What Neuroscientists Think, and Don't Think, About Consciousness.* Frontiers in Human Neuroscience. 16:767612.

Klein, G. (2015). *Seeing What Others Don't: The Remarkable Ways We Gain Insights.* PublicAffairs.

Kleon, A. (2012). *Steal Like an Artist: 10 Things Nobody Told You About Being Creative.* Workman Publishing Company.

Kuhn, T. (2012). *The Structure of Scientific Revolutions: 50th Anniversary Edition.* University of Chicago Press.

Lopata, J., Barr, N., Slayton, M. & Seli, P. (2022). *Dual-modes of creative thought in the classroom: Implications of network neuroscience for creativity education.* Translational Issues in Psychological Science, 8(1), pp. 79–89.

McIntosh R. & Della Sala, S. (2022). *The persistent irony of the Dunning-Kruger Effect.* The Psychologist (07 February 2022). https://www.bps.org.uk/psychologist/persistent-iro-ny-dunning-kruger-effect

Michael Jordan Statistics. (2022). *Michael Jordan.* Basketball Reference https://www.basketball-reference.com/players/j/jordami01.html

Michalko, M. (2006). *Thinkertoys: A Handbook of Creative-Thinking Techniques; 2nd Edition.* Ten Speed Press.

Mile Coric, D. (2021). *The importance of thought experiments.* Pravo - teorija i praska. 38, pp. 31-42.

Mohajer, S. (2015). *The Little Book of Stupidity: How We Lie to Ourselves and Don't Believe Others.* CreateSpace Independent Publishing Platform.

Mullen, B., Johnson, C. & Salas, E. (1991). *Productivity Loss in Brainstorming Groups: A Meta-Analytic Integration.*

Basic and Applied Social Psychology, 12:1, pp. 3-23.

Mullis, K. (2009). *Polymerase Chain Reaction; Making DNA accessible.* Kary Mullis personal website. https://www.karymullis.com/pcr.shtml

Naqvi, N., Shiv, B. & Bechara, A. (2006). *The Role of Emotion in Decision Making: A Cognitive Neuroscience Perspective.* Current Directions in Psychological Science, 15(5), pp. 260-264.

National Center for Health Statistics. (2022). *Marriage and Divorce.* https://www.cdc.gov/nchs/fastats/marriage-divorce.htm

Newton, I. & Hooke, R. (1675). *Isaac Newton letter to Robert Hooke.* Historical Society of Pennsylvania.

Oakley, B. (2017). *Mindshift: Break Through Obstacles to Learning and Discover Your Hidden Potential.* TarcherPerigee.

Parrish S. & Kahneman, D. (2019). *[The Knowledge Project Ep. #68] Daniel Kahneman: Putting Your Intuition on Ice.* Farnam Street Media Inc. https://fs.blog/knowledge-project-podcast-transcripts/daniel-kahneman-68/

Parrish, S. (2015) - 2022. *Inspiration from 150 episodes of The Knowledge Project with Shane Parrish.* Farnam Street Media Inc. https://fs.blog/knowledge-project-podcast/

Ries, E. (2011). *The Lean Startup: How Today's Entrepreneurs Use Continuous Innovation to Create Radically Successful Businesses.* Crown Business.

Rousseau, D. (2014). *The Oxford Handbook of Evidence-Based Management (Oxford Library of Psychology);*

1st edition. Oxford University Press.

Rowling, J. & Fry, S. (2001). *Harry Potter and Me (BBC Christmas Special, British version)* BBC, Accio Quote. http://www.accio-quote.org/articles/2001/1201-bbc-hpandme.htm

Seneca, L. (2017). *On The Tranquillity Of The Mind.* Independently Published.

Shiv, B. (2007). *Emotions, decisions, and the brain.* Journal of Consumer Psychology, 17(3), pp. 174-178.

Shiv, B. (2013). *How Do You Find Breakthrough Ideas?.* Insights by Stanford Business. https://www.gsb.stanford.edu/insights/baba-shiv-how-do-you-find-breakthrough-ideas

Shiv, B. (2021). *Lectures held for LEAD program participants.* Stanford Graduate School of Business LEAD Program.

Siegel, D. (2010). *Mindsight: The New Science of Personal Transformation.* Bantam.

Syed, M. (2015). *Black Box Thinking: Why Most People Never Learn from Their Mistakes--But Some Do.* Portfolio.

Taleb, N. (2001). *Fooled by Randomness: The Hidden Role of Chance in Life and in the Markets.* Random House.

Terninko J., Zusman, A. & Zlotin, B. (1998). *Systematic Innovation: An Introduction to TRIZ (Theory of Inventive Problem Solving); 1st Edition.* St. Lucie Press.

Tesla N. & Dunlap, O. (1934). *An inventor's seasoned ideas; Nikola Tesla, Pointing to 'Grevious Errors' of the Past,*

Explains Radio as He Sees It at Age of 77 -- He Expects Television. The New York Times.

Urban, T. (2019). *The American Brain.* WaitButWhy. https://waitbutwhy.com/2019/09/american-brain.html

Vallat R., Türker, B., Nicolas, A. & Ruby, P. (2022). *High Dream Recall Frequency is Associated with Increased Creativity and Default Mode Network Connectivity.* Nat Sci Sleep. 2022 Feb 22;14: pp. 265-275.

Wagner, U., Gais, S., Haider, H., Verleger, R. & Born, J. (2004). *Sleep inspires insight.* Nature, 427, pp. 352-355.

Ward, M. (2016). *How billionaire tech mogul Elon Musk got his start.* CNBC. https://www.cnbc.com/2016/09/02/how-billionaire-tech-mogul-elon-musk-got-his-start.html

Webb Young, J. (2003). *A Technique for Producing Ideas; 1st edition.* McGraw Hill.

Weinberg, G. & McCann, L. (2019). *Super Thinking: The Big Book of Mental Models.* Portfolio.

Wideman, R. (2013). *The As If Principle: The Radically New Approach to Changing Your Life.* Free Press.

Wikipedia community. (2022) *Banana peel, accessed on 14 August 2022.* Wikimedia Foundation. https://en.wikipedia.org/wiki/Banana_peel

Wikiquote.org community (2022). *Talk: Albert Einstein, accessed on 14 August 2022.* Wikimedia Foundation. https://en.wikiquote.org/wiki/Talk:Albert_Einstein#Unsourced_and_dubious/overly_modern_sources

Wilson, R. (2016). *Quantum Psychology: How Brain Software Programs You and Your World.* Hilaritas Press.

Witkowski, T. (2010). *Thirty-Five Years of Research on Neuro-Linguistic Programming. NLP Research Data Base. State of the Art or Pseudoscientific Decoration?*. Polish Psychological Bulletin 41 (2010): 58-66.

Young, S. (2019). *Ultralearning: Master Hard Skills, Outsmart the Competition, and Accelerate Your Career.* Harper Business.